Business and Industry

EDITORS

William R. Childs
Scott B. Martin
Wanda Stitt-Gohdes

VOLUME 9

SAVINGS AND INVESTMENT OPTIONS
to TELECOMMUTING

MARSHALL CAVENDISH
NEW YORK · TORONTO · LONDON · SYDNEY

Marshall Cavendish
99 White Plains Road
Tarrytown, New York 10591-9001

www.marshallcavendish.com

Library of Congress Cataloging-in-Publication Data

Business and industry / editors, William R. Childs, Scott B. Martin, Wanda Stitt-Gohdes.
    p. cm.
  Includes bibliographical reference and index.
  Contents: v. 1. Accounting and Bookkeeping to Burnett, Leo--v. 2. Business Cycles to Copyright--
v. 3. Corporate Governance to Entrepreneurship--v. 4. Environmentalism to Graham,
Katharine--v. 5. Great Depression to Internship--v. 6. Inventory to Merrill Lynch--
v. 7. Microeconomics to Philip Morris Companies--v. 8. Price Controls to Sarnoff, David--
v. 9. Savings and Investment Options to Telecommuting--v. 10. Temporary Workers to Yamaha--
v. 11. Index volume
    ISBN 0-7614-7430-7 (set)--ISBN 0-7614-7439-0 (v. 9)
      1. Business--Encyclopedias. 2. Industries--Encyclopedias. I. Childs, William R., 1951-II. Martin,
  Scott B., 1961-III. Stitt-Gohdes, Wanda.

HF1001 .B796 2003
338'.003--dc21   2002035156

Printed in Italy

06 05 04 03   5 4 3 2 1

MARSHALL CAVENDISH
Editorial Director   Paul Bernabeo
Production Manager   Alan Tsai

Produced by The Moschovitis Group, Inc.

THE MOSCHOVITIS GROUP
President, Publishing Division   Valerie Tomaselli
Executive Editor   Hilary W. Poole
Associate Editor   Sonja Matanovic
Design and Layout   Annemarie Redmond
Illustrator   Richard Garratt
Assistant Illustrator   Zahiyya Abdul-Karim
Photo Research   Gillian Speeth
Production Associates   K. Nura Abdul-Karim, Rashida Allen
Editorial Assistants   Christina Campbell, Nicole Cohen, Jessica Rosin
Copyediting   Carole Campbell
Proofreading   Paul Scaramazza
Indexing   AEIOU, Inc.

Alphabetical Table of Contents

Savings and Investment Options

Almost everyone dreams about becoming financially independent and retiring young. Most people do not fulfill that dream because they do not take control of their finances. The hardest part of saving money is the discipline required to do so regularly, but setting goals and developing a financial plan can provide the motivation necessary to be a successful, disciplined saver.

The question that lurks in the minds of many potential investors is "When should I start saving?" The practical answer is "yesterday." Consider the following example (shown in the chart on page 1158). Beginning at age 18, Julie contributes $1,000 per year for 10 years to an investment account that earns 10 percent interest. Julie's twin brother, John, decides to wait until he is 28 to begin saving. He contributes $1,000 per year to an account earning 10 percent from age 28 until age 65. Who will have more money at age 65? Julie will have accumulated $596,129 by age 65 even though she contributed a total of only $10,000 to her account. John will have contributed $38,000, but his account will be worth only $364,043 at age 65. Why the difference? Julie started earlier and enjoyed the benefit of more years of compound interest. As this example illustrates, the cost of waiting to begin investing is significant.

Financial Securities

The first step to successful investing is understanding the available investment choices. Investments are often referred to as financial assets or securities. Financial securities, which provide cash return, can be divided into two categories: nontradable and tradable securities. Nontradable securities include savings accounts, certificates of deposit (CDs), and other accounts offered by banks and brokerage firms. Investors can put money into and withdraw money from these accounts on demand, but they cannot sell their ownership in these accounts to another investor. Nontradable accounts are usually very low risk because they are insured by the government (Federal Deposit Insurance Corporation [FDIC]) or through private investment insurance (Securities Investor Protection Corporation).

Stocks and bonds are tradable securities; they can easily be bought and sold in public markets like the New York Stock Exchange or the Nasdaq market. Stocks, also known as equities, represent ownership in a publicly traded company. An investor who owns stock in Coca-Cola, for example, literally owns a piece of the company, has the right to vote at the company's annual meeting, and can claim a proportionate share of the company's net income. Stockholders receive their share of the company's net

See also:
Compound Interest; Finance, Personal; Mutual Funds; New York Stock Exchange; Stocks and Bonds.

Analysts say it is never too soon to start saving.

Although Julie saved less money over a shorter period of time than her twin brother, John, she ends up with far more money than John at age 65, because her savings earned compound interest over a longer period of time.

The Impact of Compound Interest

	Period of savings	Annual contribution	Total contribution at age 65	Annual interest	Age of account	Value of account
Julie	10 years	$1,000	$10,000	10%	47 years	$596,129
John	38 years	$1,000	$38,000	10%	37 years	$364,043

income as dividends. Equities (stocks) are the savings vehicle of choice for many investors. According to *Equity Ownership in America*, a 1999 study commissioned by the Investment Company Institute and the Securities Industry Association, 48 percent of U.S. households owned stock in 1999, up from only 19 percent in 1983.

Investors who own bonds are lenders, not owners; they lend money to the company that issues the bonds in return for a fixed series of combined interest and principal payments. Bondholders do not have voting rights, nor do they have a claim to the company's earnings. Bonds are referred to as debt securities.

Mutual funds, another kind of investment, became very popular in the last two decades of the twentieth century. According to the Investment Company Institute, the number of U.S. mutual funds has grown from 371 funds in 1984 to 6,965 funds in 2000. Mutual funds collect money from many investors and pool the money to purchase shares of stock in many different companies. Investors in mutual funds own shares of the fund. Each share represents ownership of a small piece of every company that the mutual fund owns. Mutual funds are ideal investment vehicles for beginning investors

because they allow for small contributions (as low as $25 per month) and provide immediate diversification (ownership of stock of companies in many industries).

Some mutual funds also invest in bonds. Money market mutual funds have become a popular alternative to savings accounts. They purchase short-term government securities, such as Treasury bills (T-bills), which are relatively safe. Unlike savings accounts, money market mutual funds are not insured by the FDIC, but they do provide higher returns than savings accounts.

Risk and Return

The return on an asset can be divided into two components, capital gains and dividends or interest. Companies pay interest to their bondholders to compensate them for lending money to the firm. Some companies distribute a portion of their earnings to stockholders (owners) by paying dividends. Capital gains occur when an asset (a stock or bond) is sold for more than its original purchase price. Bondholders receive most of their income through interest payments, but they may achieve capital gains as well. Because not all companies pay dividends, stockholders receive most of their return in the form of capital gains. Dividends, interest,

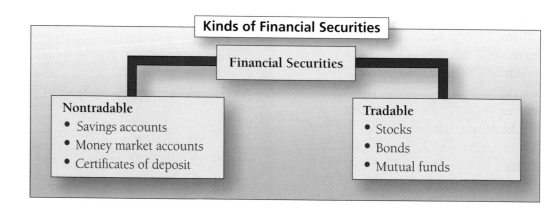

Kinds of Financial Securities

Financial Securities

Nontradable
- Savings accounts
- Money market accounts
- Certificates of deposit

Tradable
- Stocks
- Bonds
- Mutual funds

and capital gains are all taxed, but capital gains are usually taxed at a lower rate. Furthermore, the tax on capital gains is not due until the asset is sold; the tax on interest and dividends is due every year.

Different financial assets offer different amounts of return and risk, but what is a realistic return? The return that investors earn depends on the kind of security in which they invest. For example, savings accounts, which are insured by the FDIC, are virtually risk free and usually provide a return of less than 2 percent per year. To earn higher returns, investors must be willing to take on more risk. The table on the right shows average annual returns and standard deviations (in this case, a measure of risk) from 1926 to 1998 for several kinds of tradable U.S. financial assets.

The return is the reward that investors receive for bearing the risk (standard deviation) associated with each asset. More risk gives more uncertainty about future returns—the chance of losing money is greater. Assets that provide higher rates of return are usually riskier. Small-company stocks, the asset class with the highest standard deviation, provide the greatest potential reward, while T-bills, the asset class with the lowest standard deviation, provide the least potential return.

In *Stocks for the Long Run* (1998), noted economist Jeremy Siegel asserts that stocks are unquestionably riskier than bonds or T-bills in the short run. However, investing in common stocks for the long term provides a very different risk profile. Siegel studied returns from 1802 to 1997 and found that if stocks are owned for at least 10 years, they perform better than do bonds or T-bills. Furthermore, Siegel's analysis shows that for 20-year holding periods, stock return rates have never fallen behind inflation, while bonds and T-bills fell behind inflation at an average rate of 3 percent per year over 20-year periods. This evidence suggests that stocks are the safest long-term investment for investors who hope to maintain and increase their purchasing power.

To reduce risk, investors should diversify their portfolios (their array of investments).

Average Returns and Deviations 1926 to 1998		
Asset	Average Annual Return	Standard Deviation (Risk)
Large-company stocks	13.2%	20.3%
Small-company stocks	17.4%	33.8%
Long-term corporate bonds	6.1%	8.6%
Long-term government bonds	5.7%	9.2%
Short-term government bonds (T-bills)	3.8%	3.2%

Source: Ibbotson Associates Inc., *Stocks, Bonds, Bills and Inflation 1999 Yearbook*, Charlottesville, Va., Financial Associates Research Foundation, 2000.

Diversification occurs when investors divide their money among many different kinds of investment. The most basic level of diversification is buying stock in many companies rather than just one. Investors can diversify even more by purchasing different kinds of stocks, including international stocks, and adding bonds to their portfolios.

Developing a Savings and Investment Plan
Investors have the opportunity to participate in many different kinds of savings plans, either through their jobs or on their own. For example, anyone with earned income can open an Individual Retirement Account (IRA) and make annual contributions to that account. In 2002 investors were able to contribute $5,000 per year to IRA accounts. The money invested in an IRA can be used to purchase many kinds of financial assets, including stocks, bonds, and mutual funds. IRAs are of two kinds: the Roth and the Traditional IRA. The Roth IRA provides tax-free earnings, while the Traditional IRA provides tax-deferred earnings; in some cases, Traditional IRA contributions are tax deductible.

Many investors also have the opportunity to participate in retirement plans at work, including plans known as 401(k) and

Qualities of Successful Investors
1. **Disciplined:** Pay themselves first.
2. **Diversified:** Divide money among many different kinds of assets.
3. **Patient:** Leave money invested in the stock market for the long term.
4. **Proactive:** Do not wait to start investing.

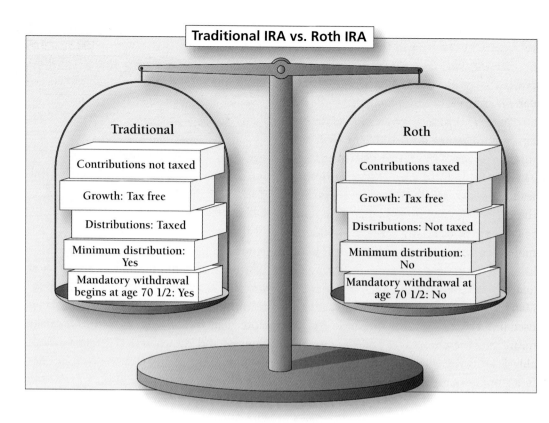

Traditional IRA vs. Roth IRA

Traditional	Roth
Contributions not taxed	Contributions taxed
Growth: Tax free	Growth: Tax free
Distributions: Taxed	Distributions: Not taxed
Minimum distribution: Yes	Minimum distribution: No
Mandatory withdrawal begins at age 70 1/2: Yes	Mandatory withdrawal at age 70 1/2: No

403(b) plans. Contributions to these plans are tax deductible, and the earnings they generate are tax-deferred until the money is withdrawn. In many cases, the employer will offer to match some of the employee's contributions to the plan, which effectively increases the employee's annual salary. Contributions to these plans are usually invested in mutual funds.

Successful investors are disciplined, diversified, patient, and proactive. Disciplined investors pay themselves first by having money deducted from every paycheck and deposited directly into their retirement plans, IRAs, or other investment accounts. Diversified investors understand that dividing their money among many different kinds of assets reduces risk and stabilizes return. Patient investors leave their money invested in the stock market for the long term. They do not try to "time the market"—pulling their money out when the stock market begins to decline. Proactive investors do not wait until next month or next year to start investing; they start now to get the maximum benefits of compound interest.

Web Resources on Savings and Investment

www.oag.state.ny.us/investors/invest_1.html provides general information on establishing a solid financial plan to ensure the ability to save and invest earnings.

www.urbanext.uiuc.edu/ww1/12-02.html is a woman's guide to saving and investing.

www.thisismoney.com/saving.html provides general information and resources on saving and investment options.

www.sec.gov/investor/cosra/brochure.htm is the SEC's Web page on general information regarding savings and investments.

www.dfi.wa.gov/sd/teens.htm is a Web site for teens on learning how to manage personal finances.

www.morningstar.com is the home page of Morningstar, a provider of mutual fund, stock, and variable annuity investment information.

Further Reading

Investing in Your Future. Mason, Ohio: South-Western Thomson Learning, 2003.

Malkiel, Burton. *A Random Walk down Wall Street.* New York: W. W. Norton, 2000.

The Motley Fool. http://www.fool.com (March 19, 2003).

Siegel, Jeremy. *Stocks for the Long-Run.* New York: McGraw-Hill, 2002.

Trivoli, George W. *Personal Portfolio Management.* Upper Saddle River, N.J.: Prentice Hall, 2000.

Vick, Timothy P. *How to Pick Stocks like Warren Buffet: Profiting from the Bargain Hunting Strategies of the World's Greatest Value Investor.* New York: McGraw-Hill, 2001.

—*Angeline Lavin*

Scarcity

Scarcity is generally thought to be the fundamental concept underlying all economic analysis. In concrete terms: people never have enough of certain things, and those things are, accordingly, considered scarce. This simple interpretation of scarcity is misleading, however. Economists understand the concept to be more far-reaching, and they apply it in subtle ways that involve more than simple enumeration.

Scarcity in Common and Technical Usage

Many key words used in economics are also used in everyday language, but the everyday meaning of these words may differ considerably from their technical meaning. *Scarcity* is a good example. Guided by common usage, dictionaries typically define *scarcity* as "a condition of being scarce." *Scarce* may then be defined as "not common, rarely seen, not plentiful." This definition suggests that to be scarce, an item or resource must not be abundant. In contrast, however, economists often speak of the scarcity of goods that do seem abundant, or they may speak of the scarcity of all resources. In societies where consumer goods exist in obvious abundance, such statements are apt to seem confusing or false.

These different uses of the term reflect that, in economics, the meaning of scarcity is always relative, not absolute. Relative to what? To what people want. A typical economics textbook defines *scarcity* as "a situation where human wants are greater than the available resources." If wants increase or decrease, then the level of scarcity can change. For example, suppose that in an underdeveloped economy people want more telephones than the economy provides. As the economy grows in its ability to provide telephones, what happens? More people may decide that they want telephones. In this case, as more telephones are produced, telephones may become, in economic terms, more scarce than they were before.

Scarcity and Choice

What makes scarcity central to the study of economics? The concept provides economists with an approach to the general task of explaining human behavior. Some economists focus on commercial activities, such as producing and consuming material goods and services; others study a wide range of noncommercial activities, including environmental protection, marriage, divorce, and other social relationships. All economists, however, concentrate on the choices people make in pursuit of their goals. These choices are driven by scarcity—or, to put it differently, scarcity creates the need for choice. Rich or poor, when people want more than they can have, they must make choices, and the choices they make shape their life in the public and private spheres.

What guides people as they weigh the alternatives in situations requiring choice? The answer, according to economists, is cost. Here again, economists use an ordinary word in a special way. Every choice involves a cost, they say, even in cases where no money is at stake. The cost is the opportunity that is lost in every act of choice. In every choice, we choose and refuse at the same time. If the choice is between spending time at work or at home with one's family, the alternative not selected is the cost of the choice. The choice is picking which cost to pay. Of course the example assumes that in this case one cannot have everything he or she wants—to work and be with the family at the same time. It also assumes that the person making the choice considers both alternatives valuable.

See also:
Cost; Environmentalism;
Opportunity Cost.

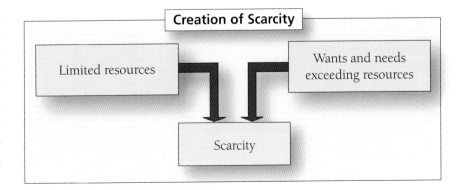

Creation of Scarcity

Limited resources → Scarcity ← Wants and needs exceeding resources

**Basic Economic Questions
Posed by Scarcity**

1. What goods should be produced?
2. How should these goods be produced?
3. For whom will these goods be produced?

Scarcity and Valuable Use

As the example above suggests, the concept of scarcity involves choices about the valuable use of a resource. Scarcity will exist in any situation where a resource has more than one valuable use. Valuable, here, means worthy of some sort of sacrifice. Consider the example of water in a river. When the water serves only one valuable use—as a place to catch fish, say—the water may seem abundant and not scarce. As no competing use for the water is present, nobody needs to choose among alternative possibilities.

What happens, however, if people also value using the river water to generate electricity via dams and power plants, or if they value using it to irrigate farmland, or to supply a distant city with drinking water? Now water becomes a scarce resource because people have alternative uses for it, and they are willing (according to their respective values) to bear the cost of converting the water from one use to another. The water may still be abundant, in the simple sense that plenty of it continues to flow along, but one valuable use of it now interferes with others. Water used for irrigation cannot be used for fish habitat, or the generation of electrical power, or supplying city taps. Thus, a choice must be made about the best use of this scarce resource.

The need for choice in these cases is sometimes regarded as unfortunate, but choice arises out of human ingenuity, which, over time, has discovered many uses for resources previously thought to have only one use or none. Such discoveries often provide for increases in human comfort and, at the same time, increased levels of scarcity. This is the kind of problematic situation, often marked by irony, that economists study, focusing on the choices people make to resolve conflicts arising from competing judgments about valuable uses of resources.

Scarcity and Abundance

Even when resources exist in abundance, issues of scarcity arise when people make choices about the use of those resources. Imagine a beach with an abundance of pebbles. Imagine also that you want some of the pebbles for use in your garden. Nobody else wants any of the pebbles, and their role in preserving the ecosystem of the beach will not be affected by the small quantity you would like to take. In this case, pebbles do not seem to be scarce. The pebbles you want to take have no valuable, alternative use. Nevertheless a scarcity issue is present. You will spend time and effort to gather the pebbles, load them into your car, and relocate them to your garden—and your time and effort are scarce. Instead of working to collect pebbles, you could engage in other valuable activities such as working at a paying job, or tending to your garden in a different way. If you collect the pebbles, you choose not to do those other things—not at the moment at least. Scarcity intrudes in such cases, regardless of the quantity of pebbles on the beach.

Acting As If Resources Were Not Scarce

In many circumstances marked by scarcity, people may fail to see the need for a choice because the resource in question is not scarce in their judgment. Here are two examples.

- Individuals traveling with an expense account that covers their travel costs, and nothing else, may spend lavishly. These travelers have only one valuable use of the funds, so the money may not seem scarce—there is no other use for it—and the travelers may feel no need to hold back on travel-related spending. By contrast, a traveler working from a fixed travel budget, with funds drawn from his or her checking account, will know that money not spent on travel can be put to other valuable uses.
- Farmers with a "use it or lose it" water irrigation contract may use all of the water allocated to them even when they do not need it all for raising their crops. The irrigation contract specifies that the farmers have only one valuable use of the water, and that they must use their entire allocation or receive less water next year. The water is still scarce in the eyes of others, relative to other valuable uses, but for the farmers it has no other use and therefore does not seem scarce.

Oxygen provides a similar example. People cannot live without oxygen, yet oxygen does not ordinarily seem scarce. It is present abundantly in the atmosphere. Divers who want oxygen in a metal tank so they can breathe under water, however, must pay people to gather the oxygen and supply it to them in a special way. To these suppliers, the materials and effort required are scarce. In paying the sellers to supply the divers with oxygen, divers employ a social and economic device to draw the sellers away from other valuable activities so that the sellers can concentrate on helping the divers swim under water.

To understand economic reasoning, one must go beyond the dictionary definition of the term *scarcity* as meaning "not plentiful." Economists use the term to denote a relative relationship between what people want and what they can have. The study of that relationship yields important insights into human behavior in business and industry and in everyday life.

Water is a scarce resource in economic terms, partly because humans have so many uses for it, from drinking to washing to irrigation.

Further Reading

Brue, Stanley L., and Donald R. Wentworth. *Economic Scenes: Theory in Today's World.* Upper Saddle River, N.J.: Prentice Hall, 1991.

Davis, James E., and Regina McCormick. *Economics: A Resource Book for Secondary Schools.* Santa Barbara, Calif.: ABC-CLIO, 1988.

McConnell, Campbell R., and Stanley L. Brue. *Economics: Principles, Problems, and Policies.* 14th ed. New York: McGraw-Hill, 1999.

—*Don Wentworth*

Schumpeter, Joseph A.

1883–1950
Economist

Joseph Schumpeter is a major figure in the history of twentieth-century economic thought. Born in Austria-Hungary, Schumpeter entered Vienna University in 1901 and obtained his doctor of law degree in 1906. He then began a career as a university teacher and economic consultant. In 1919 he was appointed finance minister in the Austrian government, but he resigned within the year when he could not win approval for his monetary policy. After a spell in banking and work in a variety of teaching posts, in 1925 he accepted a chair in public finance at the University of Bonn. In 1932 he immigrated to America for a professorship at Harvard, where he taught for the remainder of his life.

Economist Joseph Schumpeter in an undated photograph.

Schumpeter's academic reputation rests on three major works: *The Theory of Economic Development* (1912), *Business Cycles* (1939), and *Capitalism, Socialism, and Democracy* (1942). Through these books he developed his famously paradoxical thesis that capitalism would be destroyed by its own successes and would evolve into a form of socialism. In *The Theory of Economic Development*, Schumpeter investigates the origin of capitalist profits. He concludes that pioneering innovators, whom he terms "entrepreneurs," create profits by introducing technological or organizational changes that result in either the more efficient production of existing goods and services or in the development of new ones. Without entrepreneurs a capitalist economy would reach static equilibrium, with zero net growth. Yet only a minority of capitalists are entrepreneurs. Most only imitate and incorporate entrepreneurial innovations, thereby eliminating the competitive advantages of those innovations, causing investment to fall, and possibly inducing a downturn in the trade cycle.

Schumpeter maintained a career-long interest in such periodic economic fluctuations. In *Business Cycles*, he draws on the work of the Russian economist N. D. Kondratiev to explain cycles of various durations. Writing against the background of the Great Depression, Schumpeter insists on the long-term economic viability of capitalism but warns that the system is endangered by social factors. This argument presages the theme of what is generally taken to be his masterpiece.

Schumpeter's argument in *Capitalism, Socialism, and Democracy* is that capitalism's economic success has undermined the social and cultural prerequisites of continued success. As a dynamic system, capitalism relies on perpetual change though "creative destruction," driven by an animating spirit of entrepreneurship. However, this spirit is stifled by the growth of centralized and bureaucratic corporations, where salaried employees have little opportunity to contribute in original ways to the development of the business. Successful capitalist societies also tend to produce a skeptical intelligentsia, with sufficient

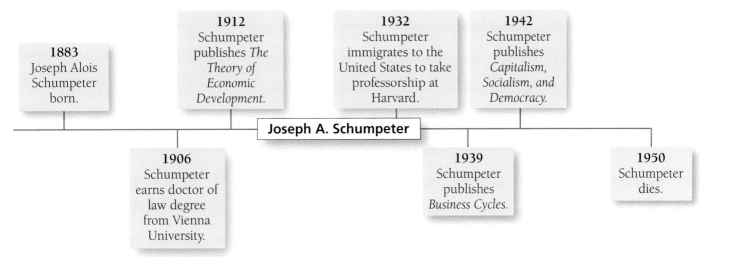

1883
Joseph Alois Schumpeter born.

1912
Schumpeter publishes *The Theory of Economic Development.*

1932
Schumpeter immigrates to the United States to take professorship at Harvard.

1942
Schumpeter publishes *Capitalism, Socialism, and Democracy.*

Joseph A. Schumpeter

1906
Schumpeter earns doctor of law degree from Vienna University.

1939
Schumpeter publishes *Business Cycles.*

1950
Schumpeter dies.

leisure to critique capitalist values and to develop informed interests in alternative socioeconomic systems. Under these conditions, Schumpeter argues, capitalism's "heir apparent" is a form of managerial socialism.

As its title implies, Schumpeter's 1942 work is concerned not only with capitalism and socialism but also with democracy. He argues that the classical democratic ideal erroneously presupposes an informed and engaged citizenry. In reality, Schumpeter maintains, political understanding is confined to a small elite that achieves power through "a competitive struggle for the people's vote." In Schumpeter's analysis, democracy is demoted from a way of life to a mere mechanism.

Now a neglected classic, *Capitalism, Socialism, and Democracy* provides an important analysis of its own time. Schumpeter also correctly observed that capitalism had begun to lose its legitimacy in the eyes of Western intellectuals. Many post–World War II theoreticians, for example, Herbert Marcuse in *One-Dimensional Man* (1964), went on to denounce the values of capitalist society in much the way Schumpeter had earlier envisaged.

Schumpeter's economic analysis has lost credibility for two reasons: the communist system has given way to capitalism, rather than vice versa, and the information revolution of the late twentieth century came from entrepreneurs operating not in bureaucratic corporations but in new and small businesses. Schumpeter's political analysis, by contrast,

has proven to be more enduring: *Capitalism, Socialism, and Democracy* paved the way for the "rational choice" school of political science, according to which political actors (politicians, voters, lobbyists, and so on) rationally pursue their self-interests within the political system, just as producers and consumers pursue their interests in the marketplace.

Further Reading

Moss, Laurence S., ed. *Joseph A. Schumpeter, Historian of Economics.* London: Routledge, 1996.

Schumpeter, Joseph A. *Business Cycles: A Theoretical, Historical, and Statistical Analysis of the Capitalist Process.* 1959. Reprint, Philadelphia: Porcupine Press, 1982.

———. *Capitalism, Socialism, and Democracy.* 1942. Reprint, London: Unwin Paperbacks, 1987.

Swedberg, Richard. *Schumpeter: A Biography.* Princeton, N.J.: Princeton University Press, 1991.

—*Peter C. Grosvenor*

[T]he history of the productive apparatus of a typical farm, from the beginnings of the rationalization of crop rotation, plowing and fattening to the mechanized thing of today—linking up with elevators and railroads—is a history of revolutions. So is the history of the productive apparatus of the iron and steel industry from the charcoal furnace to our own type of furnace, or the history of the apparatus of power production from the overshot water wheel to the modern power plant, or the history of transportation from the mailcoach to the airplane. The opening up of new markets, foreign or domestic, and the organizational development from the craft shop and factory to such concerns as U.S. Steel illustrate the same process of industrial mutation—if I may use that biological term—that incessantly revolutionizes the economic structure from within, incessantly destroying the old one, incessantly creating a new one. This process of Creative Destruction is the essential fact about capitalism. It is what capitalism consists in and what every capitalist concern has got to live in.

—Joseph Schumpeter, *Capitalism, Socialism, and Democracy,* 1942

See also:
Savings and Investment Options; Stocks and Bonds.

Schwab, Charles

1937–
Stockbroker, entrepreneur

Charles Schwab did more to democratize the business of stock trading than any single person in the industry. Taking on the powerful and restrictive brokerages that permitted only established clients to trade stocks and then charged them commissions based on a percentage of the trade, Schwab simplified the trading process and drastically reduced the cost of buying and selling stocks. In opening up Wall Street investment to anyone who could pick up a phone, Schwab gave regular people easy access to the world of investing.

Charles Schwab was born in Sacramento, California, in 1937. Ever the entrepreneur, Schwab sold walnuts as a youngster, eschewing the common black walnuts for the rarer English walnuts that fetched a better price. At age 12 he switched to selling eggs and then moved into selling the chickens themselves, along with fertilizer made by mixing their droppings with straw. The work was hard, the days were long, and he ultimately sold the business (at a profit, he says) to become a caddy. On the golf course, Schwab learned a lifelong lesson about the importance of the relationship between his earnings and his customers' satisfaction.

Schwab had always had reading problems; in his 30s, he was finally diagnosed as dyslexic. Schwab struggled with the written word but was a master of math and science. Accepted to Stanford University, he continued to have problems with reading—he failed freshman English and French—so he threw his energy into the courses where he could do well. He received a bachelor of arts in economics in 1959 and a master of business administration from Stanford Graduate School of Business in 1961.

Schwab founded his own brokerage firm in 1971 but was only mildly successful until the 1975 government deregulation of brokerage fees. With their rates no longer under government control, most brokerage houses took advantage of their customers and raised their rates. Charles Schwab and Company did just the opposite. It set up a customer-friendly operation that featured low, fixed fees and 24-hour service. In doing so, the firm welcomed a whole new class of investors who could complete a transaction for an unheard-of price of $30.

Recalling the condescending and unsympathetic attitude of the brokers he had encountered as a young adult investor, Schwab set out to put the customer's interests first. His elimination of percentage

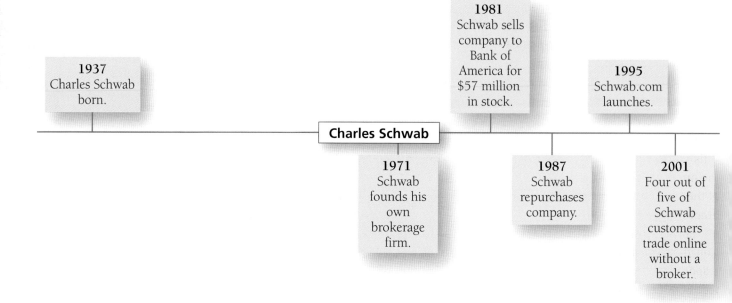

1937
Charles Schwab born.

1971
Schwab founds his own brokerage firm.

1981
Schwab sells company to Bank of America for $57 million in stock.

1987
Schwab repurchases company.

1995
Schwab.com launches.

2001
Four out of five of Schwab customers trade online without a broker.

Charles Schwab

commissions was only the first action he took on behalf of the customer. Nine years later, when newer discount brokers became competitors, Charles Schwab took another step to innovate. This time the company opened a supermarket of mutual funds for its customers and followed that with free IRA accounts.

Bucking the trends of the status quo by selling stocks for less profit than the established brokerages made Schwab and Company unpopular in traditional financial circles. As a result, when Schwab went seeking badly needed capital in the 1980s, the big brokerages turned him down. Schwab was forced to sell his company to the Bank of America; the sale was completed in 1981 for $57 million in stock, but Schwab was able to repurchase the company in 1987 via a friendly $280 million leveraged buyout. Schwab went public that same year, at a market value of well over $400 million. By 1990 Schwab and Company was the largest discount brokerage firm in the United States.

Schwab was one of the first in his field to recognize the importance of the Internet. The Web site Schwab.com was launched in 1995 and was among the first to offer online trades. Before 1995 all Schwab's transactions were done by phone or at one of its 377 branches. By January 2001 four of five clients were trading online with no assistance whatsoever from a Schwab agent.

Another challenge facing Schwab was to extract itself from its difficult position in the brokerage industry. On the low end, start-up discount brokers were undercutting Schwab's prices—charging as little as $8 and $10 per trade. At the other end of the spectrum, large brokerages offered in-depth market analyses, personal service, and initial public offerings to their wealthy clients. This competition left Schwab stranded in the middle without the appeal and services of the high-end firms or the low rates of the other discounters.

Staying true to his beliefs that competition dictates change and the best change response is always improved customer service, Schwab launched a media initiative

Charles Schwab in his company's computer room in 1981.

with America Online. Designed to convert, inform, and retain its customers, this undertaking included a Signature Service designed to appeal to high-end investors. The success of the multifaceted media campaign, which included television ads and video interviews presented on the Web site, can be attributed to Charles Schwab himself. Portrayed as the champion of the individual investor and a neutral source of Wall Street information,

A computer monitor displays the Chinese version of Charles Schwab's online trading Web site.

Schwab appears as a genuine but polished and levelheaded individual. His face welcomes visitors to the Schwab Web site, his mellifluous voice guiding newcomers through it, step-by-step.

Another noteworthy Charles Schwab, the respected industrialist who brokered the merger between J. P. Morgan and Andrew Carnegie to form U. S. Steel and later Bethlehem Steel in the early 1900s, was said to be able to "talk the legs off a brass pot." The contemporary Charles Schwab (no relation) follows in the footsteps of the former, using a similar convincing banter to influence individual investors and financial players alike.

Further Reading

Kador, John. *Charles Schwab: How One Company Beat Wall Street and Reinvented the Brokerage Industry.* Hoboken, N.J.: J. Wiley, 2002.

Kahn, Joseph. "Schwab Lands Feet First on Net." *New York Times,* 10 February 1999.

Kover, Amy. "Schwab Makes a Grand Play for the Rich." *Fortune,* 7 February 2000.

Malkiel, Burton. *A Random Walk down Wall Street.* New York: W. W. Norton, 2002.

Mayer, Martin. *Stealing the Market.* New York: Basic Books, 1993.

Schwab, Charles. *Charles Schwab's Guide to Financial Independence.* New York: Crown Publishers, 1998.

———. *How to Be Your Own Stockbroker.* New York: Macmillan, 1985.

—*Karen Ehrle*

Screen Actors Guild

The Screen Actors Guild (SAG) is the labor union of the stars, advocating for fair labor practices for actors since 1933. From the movies to television to interactive video games, virtually all screen actors in America, world-famous or struggling extras, are members of SAG.

Formed in secret amid the antilabor climate of Hollywood during the 1930s, SAG's founding members, including its first president, Ralph Morgan, sought to gain fair wages and better working conditions for all actors. The members hoped to reform the studio system, wherein actors had little control over their careers and felt, as one founding member described it, like "balls in a roulette wheel." The studio system usually offered actors only seven-year unbreakable contracts, while others were offered no contracts at all, working as weekly freelance actors or day players. Actors then were prohibited from switching studios; they could not choose their roles; and they worked unrestricted hours with no required meal breaks.

Although SAG became a member, or affiliated union, of the American Federation of Labor in 1935, not until 1937 did the motion picture studios accept SAG as a bargaining agent. Before the studios signed their first contracts with SAG, however, thousands of performers had joined.

SAG and its members weathered a political firestorm in the late 1940s and 1950s. The House Un-American Activities Committee (HUAC; a congressional committee known for its aggressive investigations of alleged subversive activities early in the cold war) set its sights on Hollywood, searching for actors and other entertainment industry members with communist leanings. In 1947, 10 producers, directors, and screenwriters, who became known as the Hollywood Ten, appeared at a hearing before HUAC and refused to answer questions about their political affiliations. Several actors, including SAG board member Gene Kelly, board member Humphrey Bogart, and his wife, Lauren Bacall, attended these congressional hearings as part of the Committee for the First Amendment. Despite this show of support for the witnesses, the Hollywood Ten served time in prison for contempt of Congress and were later fired by studio heads for refusing to cooperate with HUAC.

In response to pressure arising from HUAC and other sources, in 1947 SAG

See also:
Arts and Entertainment Industry; Labor Union; Taft–Hartley Act.

Screen Actors Guild

1933
Screen Actors Guild founded.

1947
The Hollywood Ten are called before the House Un-American Activities Committee.

1947–1952 and 1959–1960
Ronald Reagan serves as SAG president.

1969
SAG creates Ethnic Minorities Committee.

1982
SAG helps pass legislation to help actors receive auto insurance.

2000
Commercial actors go on strike for six months to protect residual payments from national ads.

What Is a Guild?

A guild is an association of people with a common interest, created for the mutual aid of its members. Although many kinds of guilds have been formed, the early merchant and craftworker guilds have proved to be the most important, with the latter considered to be the forerunners of modern trade unions.

Early guilds have been traced back to early Germanic brotherhoods, but guilds did not flourish in Europe until around 1000 C.E. As early as 700, however, guilds were firmly established in some cities of the Near East, including Constantinople, present-day Istanbul, Turkey.

Merchants organized guilds to protect their members during travel and to gain common privileges and greater profits. Guild members set prices, wages, and standards of quality for their wares. They bought large quantities of goods cheaply and controlled the market for selling. By 1200, especially in France, Germany, and the Netherlands, merchant guilds were powerful in town governments and often contributed to church and town projects.

Craftworkers—goldsmiths and carpenters, for example—also formed guilds. Craft guild members set standards of quality for their goods, controlled production quantities, and endeavored to distribute business evenly among members. Those who knew their craft well and owned their own shops were masters; highly skilled workers employed and paid by these masters were journeymen; young men learning a craft from masters were apprentices, receiving housing and meals in compensation for their work.

The medieval guilds had lost their political and economic power by the 1600s. Modern guilds like the Screen Actors Guild provide a wide range of services for mobile workers, helping free agents meet financial and social needs outside of traditional full-time jobs.

adopted a rule requiring its officers to sign affidavits confirming that they were not communists in compliance with the Taft–Hartley Act, a federal law that regulated union activity. In 1953 96 percent of SAG members voted to require an anticommunist loyalty oath of all actors joining SAG.

In 1969 the guild established an Ethnic Minorities Committee in response to actors who protested that Hollywood films stereotyped and misrepresented people of color. In 1982 this committee was renamed the Ethnic Equal Opportunities Committee; its stated purpose was to ensure and safeguard the rights and interests of ethnic minority SAG members, particularly regarding hiring practices. SAG also formed a Women's Committee to address allegations of an inequitable pay scale, negative portrayals of women in films, and sexual harassment in the industry. By 1973 SAG had dropped the anticommunist loyalty oath as a membership requirement.

In 1947 a group of SAG members calling themselves the Committee for the First Amendment (led by Lauren Bacall and Humphrey Bogart) went to Washington, D.C., to protest on behalf of the Hollywood Ten.

With the development of each new entertainment medium—television, cable, video, and computer software that incorporates live action—new areas of employment have opened up for actors, and SAG has continued to advocate for their interests. Disagreements about residual payments for films shown on television, per-use payments for television commercials, and contract terms for cable and videocassette productions have led to lawsuits, strikes, and walkouts initiated by SAG.

SAG has also gotten involved in issues outside the studio world. In 1982, for example, SAG helped get California state legislation passed that made illegal the denial of auto insurance because of an actor's occupation. The guild has won legal victories for actors to receive unemployment insurance and has fought for state privacy legislation to safeguard actors from intrusive fans. SAG now offers its members a credit union, a pension fund, a health care plan, and a scholarship program. These services are available to members who earn the minimum required amount per year through union acting jobs.

James Cagney, Charlton Heston, Edward Asner, and Patty Duke are among the many actors who have served as SAG president. Ronald Reagan was SAG president from 1947 to 1952 and from 1959 to 1960. Reagan later gave up acting for politics; he was elected governor of California and then elected to two terms as president of the United States.

SAG is a nonprofit corporation funded primarily by its members with officers serving on a volunteer basis. The guild neither contributes to nor participates in partisan politics. Although SAG offers workshops and acting courses from time to time, most of its resources are spent enforcing the contracts under which its members work. In 2000 both SAG and the American Federation of Film and Television Actors went on strike over a proposed elimination of residual payments to actors who appear in national television commercials. After a six-month strike, advertisers agreed to retain residual payments.

From its clandestine beginnings in a one-room office in 1935, SAG has grown to a current membership of approximately 90,000. It employs hundreds of staff members at six national offices and 20 branches throughout the United States. Its mission remains the development of employment opportunities for actors and the effort to protect and enforce fair labor practices throughout the entertainment industry.

Actors Paul Newman, left, Susan Sarandon, right, and Richard Dreyfuss, bottom left, at a rally in support of the strike by the Screen Actors Guild and the American Federation of Television and Radio Artists commercial actors in 2000.

Further Reading

Prindle, David F. *The Politics of Glamour: Ideology and Democracy in the Screen Actors Guild.* Madison: University of Wisconsin Press, 1988.

Vaughn, Stephen. *Ronald Reagan in Hollywood: Movies and Politics.* Cambridge: Cambridge University Press, 1994.

—*Barbara Gerber*

See also:

Great Depression; Investment; Nasdaq; New York Stock Exchange; Stocks and Bonds.

Securities and Exchange Commission

The Securities and Exchange Commission (SEC) is the federal agency that oversees securities dealers and markets and firms that issue stocks and bonds. The main goals of this agency are to promote disclosure of important information, enforce the securities laws, and protect investors. The SEC was formed in 1934 as a way to help the financial markets to recover during the Great Depression and to improve the overall conduct of securities dealers.

The SEC was formed to restore investor confidence following the stock market crash of 1929. Prior to the crash, few rules addressed the issuing and trading of securities. For example, businesses issuing stocks or bonds could legally make false or misleading statements about their operations or fail to disclose potential risks investors might face. Similarly, brokers or dealers were able to use insider information to manipulate stock prices. Although this lack of regulation created opportunities for mismanagement and fraud, shareholders generally were unconcerned because the economy and stock market appeared to be strong for most of the 1920s.

For the first nine months of 1929, stock prices had risen sharply, fueled by the use of borrowed money to buy stocks. In October the stock market bubble finally burst, and within two months, the aggregate value of the New York Stock Exchange had fallen from $89 billion to $71 billion. By 1932 the market was down more than 80 percent from its 1929 highs. For individual investors, the collapse in stock prices wiped out personal savings and brought ruin to millions. Of the $50 billion in new securities offered during the 1920s, nearly half were to become worthless.

The stock market crash had other serious repercussions. Banks lost great sums of money because they had made loans to investors to buy stock, while also investing heavily themselves. People feared that banks might not be able to pay back the money deposited in accounts and a run on the banking system ensued. Many banks closed—their depositors lost funds in their accounts. The situation became so serious that in March 1933, newly elected president Franklin D. Roosevelt declared a bank holiday (he closed the banks) and called Congress into special session to address the crisis.

One requirement to achieve economic recovery was to restore the public's faith in the capital markets. In response Congress passed the Securities Act of 1933, followed by the passage of the Securities Exchange Act of 1934, which created the SEC. These two laws were the foundation of federal regulation of securities issuers and securities markets. Under the 1933 law, companies offering securities to the public must provide all potential investors with a prospectus,

Divisions of the Securities and Exchange Commission			
Division of Market Regulation	**Division of Corporation Finance**	**Division of Investment Management**	**Division of Enforcement**
Establishes rules for securities brokers and markets; oversees Securities Investor Protection Corporation.	Collects and reviews documents that companies are required to file with SEC.	Oversees investment management industry.	Investigates possible securities law violations.

a document that contains accurate and complete financial information about their businesses, the securities they are selling, and the risks involved in investing.

The 1934 law expanded the regulatory authority of the federal government by requiring brokers, dealers, and securities exchanges to register with the SEC. It also established prohibitions on the practice of using insider information to trade in stocks, and protected shareholders by creating rules concerning the use of tender offers and proxy solicitations. Finally, all publicly held companies with more than $10 million in assets or 500 owners were required to file annual and quarterly financial statements with the SEC. These provisions were intended to force people who sell and trade securities to put investors' interests first.

The SEC consists of five commissioners who serve for five years—all five are appointed by the president; the president also designates one of these commissioners as the chair. To ensure that the commission is nonpartisan, no more than three commissioners may belong to the same political party. The work of the SEC is conducted through four divisions. The Division of

Market Regulation establishes rules for the securities brokers and markets, and it also oversees the Securities Investor Protection Corporation (SIPC), a private, nonprofit corporation that insures the securities and cash in the customer accounts of member brokerage firms against the failure of those firms. The Division of Corporation Finance collects and reviews documents (for example, annual reports) that publicly held companies are required to file with the SEC; the Division of Investment Management oversees and regulates the $15 trillion investment management industry, which includes mutual funds and investment

Harvey Pitt, then chairman of the SEC, appears before the Senate Banking, Housing, and Urban Affairs Committee in March 2002 to discuss issues raised by the collapse of Enron. Sen. Christopher Dodd, D–Conn., is at left and Sen. Paul Sarbanes, D–Md., the committee chairman, is center.

Securities and Exchange Commission   1173

It goes without saying that . . . confidence in the U.S. corporate and financial industries has been seriously eroded. The incredible growth of the 1990s made the stock market an attractive option for millions of Americans who had never invested before. Many people were given the impression that the stock market was just a game that, if played right, guaranteed tremendous returns. Many people on the inside became obsessed with share price rather than sound operations and good corporate governance, which seemed irrelevant for the short-term success of their stock.

As the bull market of the nineties began to subside, we were hit by two unexpected events. The attacks of September 11 made the entire country, including the markets, take notice of our own vulnerability. Then, beginning with the revelations of wrongdoing at Enron, the weaknesses in corporate America that had been overlooked or ignored came to light. We witnessed startling revelations of corporate fraud and corruption as well as failures in our systems of disclosure and corporate governance. As the markets reacted, many investors, and sadly, particularly small investors, saw their savings disappear, along with their dreams for the future.

As we move forward, restoring the confidence of investors and the integrity of the markets is the responsibility of us all. As you know, this is no simple task, and it cannot be achieved overnight. Investor confidence is intangible. There is no statistic that can accurately tabulate it, no measuring stick to keep track of its growth. There is no single piece of legislation or rule that can send the signal to America that all the problems have been fixed, and it's completely safe to get back in the market. . . .

In order to do this, those at the helm will have to make a conscious decision that ethics and integrity should be at the heart of every business decision. They will have to decide that the limits of the law are not the only way to determine what's right and wrong. By making this decision and demonstrating their commitment to good governance, they will set a tone that will filter down through their entire organizations. At the same time, this spirit should emanate from the bottom up. In effect, every layer of a company and its advisors must hold the others to this high standard. But, each individual will have to make this decision to go beyond the law on his or her own. We cannot legislate it or promulgate rules to enforce it. While there seems to be no shortage of headlines about corporate misdeeds and greed, we must remember that there are many good and honest people in American business who have consistently tried to make decisions for the benefit of their employees and their shareholders. Unfortunately, this environment has made them hesitant to speak out. As Chairman, I will encourage them to stand up and join the call for a reinvigoration of ethics and integrity in the business world. We need others to follow their example.

—William H. Donaldson, chairman, Securities and Exchange Commission, February 28, 2003

advisers. Finally, the Division of Enforcement investigates possible violations of securities law and refers civil violations to the courts for adjudication.

The SEC has become very influential in strengthening business practices and corporate accountability for shareholders. One area in which this agency has had a strong effect is accounting. Because the SEC has the authority to prescribe the form and content of financial statements, the agency has worked with the accounting profession to establish uniform financial accounting practices and auditing procedures. Similarly, the SEC's reporting requirements have forced managers, accountants, and attorneys to ensure accuracy as a way to avoid legal liabilities.

Since the 1980s the increase in the number of individual investors and the overall value of the stock markets has tested the effectiveness of the SEC on a number of fronts. Following the plunge in stock prices in October 1987, the SEC instituted new rules designed to limit market volatility. Another area of concern of the SEC involves monitoring of securities issued by companies operating in new business sectors, for instance, high technology. For example, the expansion of the Internet created a surge of new companies, the so-called dot-com firms, many of which had investment risks that were difficult to determine. Confidence in the Internet caused the dot-com stocks to surge in value during the late 1990s, but when these companies failed to generate profits, their subsequent collapse in 1999 and 2000 contributed to a broader loss in confidence in the markets.

Finally, the trend toward deregulation has placed a greater burden on the SEC to ensure that deregulated companies continue to operate in the public interest. The bankruptcy of Enron in 2001, which resulted in part from improper accounting practices and incomplete financial disclosure, cost investors billions and forced a major inquiry into modern securities and accounting practices that will result in a larger role for the SEC in monitoring accounting and reporting standards.

Further Reading

De Bedts, Ralph F. *The New Deal's SEC: The Formative Years*. New York: Columbia University Press, 1964.

Seligman, Joel. *The Transformation of Wall Street: A History of the Securities and Exchange Commission and Modern Corporate Finance*. Boston: Northeastern University Press, 1995.

Skousen, K. Fred. *An Introduction to the SEC*. 5th ed. Cincinnati, Ohio: South-Western, 1991.

—David Mason

Security Industry

The security industry aims to protect assets and provide a stable, nonthreatening environment where businesses and people can work without disruption or harm. The industry involves a wide range of products, services, and procedures to prevent and manage incidents caused by criminal action, natural disasters, and human error. Security can include armored vehicles, guard dogs, convex mirrors, firewalls, and infrared thermal technology devices; protocol for handling unwelcome visitors and crises; due diligence by businesses and individuals and other kinds of investigative techniques for incidents like cyber crime and financial fraud. These various aspects of security can be broken down into physical security; information security; personnel security; and information systems security.

Physical security addresses the protection of people, property, and facilities through the use of environmental design, security systems, and security guards. Such protection could include landscaping techniques, for example, the use of low, neatly trimmed bushes to create clear lines of sight; architectural elements like bright, strategically placed outdoor lighting to discourage lurkers; and devices like alarms, locks, access control, and surveillance systems.

Information security involves the protection of sensitive information, which could include intellectual property and proprietary, contractual, or personal data. Important decisions about information security include who should have access to the data, and how should data be shared and disseminated.

Personnel security focuses on the integrity and safety of an organization's workforce. Protections include security clearance procedures and other information access controls, as well as preemployment screening techniques, for example, background investigations and substance abuse testing.

See also:
Computer Industry; Defense Industry; Industrial Espionage; Information Technology.

A bulletproof aluminum car was introduced by the Brink's Express Company in 1937 for making pickups at banks.

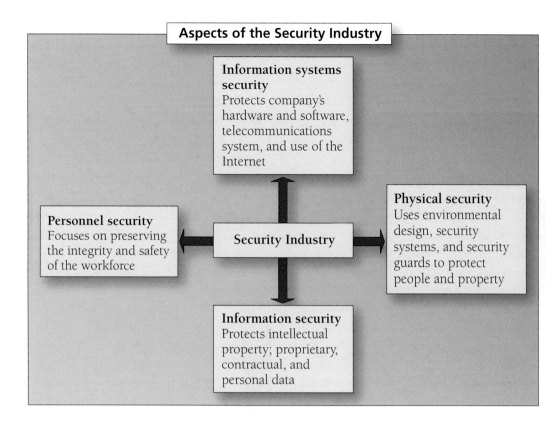

Aspects of the Security Industry

Information systems security
Protects company's hardware and software, telecommunications system, and use of the Internet

Personnel security
Focuses on preserving the integrity and safety of the workforce

Security Industry

Physical security
Uses environmental design, security systems, and security guards to protect people and property

Information security
Protects intellectual property; proprietary, contractual, and personal data

Information systems security includes the administrative, organizational, and physical measures surrounding a computer's hardware and software, a company's telecommunications systems, and the use of the Internet.

Short History of the Security Industry

The need for security is as ancient as the need to protect oneself. Physical security measures like moats, living on cliffs, and the Great Wall of China evolved over time into legislation on the practices of crime prevention and, consequently, the creation of police forces and detective businesses. In colonial America, constables and town watchmen were the primary form of security until private railroad police were established to protect goods and passengers from train robbers.

Allan Pinkerton was the first law enforcement officer hired to protect the railroads. He was also the first to establish a private detective firm, which evolved into one of the country's largest security companies. The origin of the term *private eye* can probably be traced to Pinkerton; when Pinkerton started his company in 1850, the company slogan was "We Never Sleep" and its logo was an open eye. Early on, Pinkerton hired Kate Warner, the first woman in the United States to become a detective. Around the same time, Washington Perry Brink established armored car and courier services. Brink, the company name, has long been synonymous with armored vehicles and is, at publication, the country's largest armored car company.

The growth of the security industry was stimulated by the world wars and a changing economy. Greater emphasis was placed on security in government and industrial plants; the number of government regulations was

Careers in the Security Industry

Security businesses offer various combinations of services and products including specialized services for specific industries, wide-ranging services to various industries, or particular products. Careers in the industry may include guards, armed couriers, central alarm respondents, and dog handlers.

One of the most common security careers is that of the investigator, who may have been in the military or have a background in accounting, the law, or information technology, or have industry experience in areas like retail, construction, or insurance. Investigations are conducted in response to suspected or actual incidents of sexual harassment, workplace violence, life insurance and workers' compensation fraud, product liability, arson, use of illegal telephone equipment, computer-related activity, money laundering, theft, unethical business conduct, property crime, kidnapping, and terrorism.

continually increasing; and the public police could not respond to every private need. Businesses began to form their own in-house security services instead of contracting for services from private agencies. By the 1990s security had become a multibillion-dollar industry.

Trends in the Security Industry

Prior to the terrorist attacks in New York City and near Washington, D.C., on September 11, 2001, the security industry was perceived to consist mainly of security guards, alarm systems, and surveillance equipment. In the late twentieth century growing emphasis was placed on employee screening, as organizations became more concerned with increasing incidents of workplace violence, computer hacking, and white-collar crime. These issues continue to be important and will continue to be addressed; however, the terrorist attacks on the United States suddenly awakened the nation to the idea that a previously unimaginable, highly unlikely incident was now to be considered a realistic threat. Businesses quickly reevaluated their procedures, systems, and environments. New attention was directed at high-profile buildings, airports, border and immigration patrol, and nuclear facilities. Both laypeople and experts were discussing the different forms of bioterrorism and how prepared the country was for these kinds of attack.

September 11 caused a heightened focus on enhanced electronic devices. Research and development in this area already were well under way. Devices like smart cards and smart homes, for example, are being widely considered for possible roles in securing the public and private sectors. A national identification card, or smart card, would contain personal identification information that would be accessed through a centralized source. Smart homes are homes with security systems that can be controlled from anywhere in the world using dial-in technology.

Another cutting-edge technology is biometrics—the automated capturing of a

physiological or behavioral characteristic to verify the identity of an individual. This may include fingerprints, voice patterns, iris and retinal patterns, hand geometry, signature verification, and keystroke analysis. This technology is of great concern to civil liberties activists, who worry about the possible invasion of privacy. Nevertheless, both biometrics and high-tech gadgets like smart cards are likely to play significant roles in the security industry of the future.

A palm-reading security system at the Detroit Lions indoor practice field in Allen Park, Michigan, in 2002.

Further Reading

Fay, John J., ed. *Encyclopedia of Security Management: Techniques and Technology.* Boston: Butterworth-Heinemann, 1993.

Fischer, Robert J., and Gion Green. *Introduction to Security.* Boston: Butterworth-Heinemann, 1998.

—*Lynne Bernstein*

See also:
Economies of Scale; Human Capital; Information Revolution; Manufacturing Industry; Productivity.

Service Economy

One definition of services is that they are based on a relationship, such as attorney to client, rather than on the sale of objects such as chairs.

The United States is often described as having a service economy, or an economy in which the majority of employment and business revenues are generated by services, as opposed to manufacturing or agriculture. The United States is not alone; the wealthy countries of Europe and Asia are also service economies. Indeed, many economists see a natural transition to services as countries become wealthier: poor countries rely on agriculture, better-off countries rely on manufacturing, and wealthy countries rely on services.

If a service economy is defined as one where the majority of employment is in the service sector, then the United States developed a service economy during the 1950s. The importance of the service sector has only grown: in 1960 more than 55 percent of the workforce was employed in the service sector; by 2000 that number was more than 70 percent. During the 1970s, a period of economic stagnation, some observers wondered if a service economy was a "no-growth" economy. The 1980s was a decade of low productivity gains, and some argued that improving productivity in a service economy was next to impossible. During the 1990s, as the gap between rich and poor increased, some fingered the service economy as the culprit.

The increasing importance of the service sector has created significant issues for policy makers and economists who fall back on strategies and theories developed during the industrial era. For example, a common approach for federal governments seeking to boost their economies is to reduce the amount of taxes companies pay when they make major capital investments in their businesses. However, a service economy is less capital intensive—it relies less on expensive factories and machinery—than is a manufacturing economy, so the effect of such a tax reduction may be muted. The erosion of the U.S. industrial base that has accompanied the rise of the service economy has also caused considerable distress for some workers, as manufacturers have relocated factories abroad and well-paying, often unionized, manufacturing jobs held by older workers have been lost.

What Is a Service Economy?

Considerable confusion exists about what the service economy is and how it works. No official or traditional definition of services exists. In fact, services were once regularly defined by what they are not: any

activity that does not qualify as manufacturing or agriculture is in the service sector. By this definition, services became the category for "everything else" that is happening in an economy.

When "everything else" has been the fastest-growing segment of the economy for decades, however, more precise definitions are needed. One definition of the service sector is that it produces immaterial objects. As one magazine put it, a service can be bought or sold, but it cannot be dropped on the floor. Services can have results that are quite material, however. For example, a haircut cannot be dropped on the floor, but a person who gets a haircut will notice tangible difference in his hair.

Thus, a second definition of the service sector is that service produces a change in the condition of a good or a person. A man who hires a barber to cut his hair has changed the condition of his hair. A man who hires a lawyer to get him a divorce has changed his marital condition.

Both definitions point to a peculiar issue for policy makers and economists: services are very hard to measure. A factory worker produces a certain number of goods, which can be counted. A farm likewise produces a specific amount of grain or milk that can easily be measured. How should the output of a hairdresser be measured? Weighing the hair or counting the haircuts misses an essential aspect of what makes the service—the haircut—worth buying. A doctor may see many patients, but if they all die from preventable causes, the doctor is not adequately performing medical services. As a result, some observers have called for new methods of measuring the worth of a business and its output, but little consensus exists on what those new methods should be.

Yet another definition of services is that a service produces a relation—doctor–patient, lawyer–client—rather than a thing. Defining services in this way suggests that communication is more important in a service economy than in an industrial economy because two people generally need to interact to produce a relation. It also suggests that the consumer

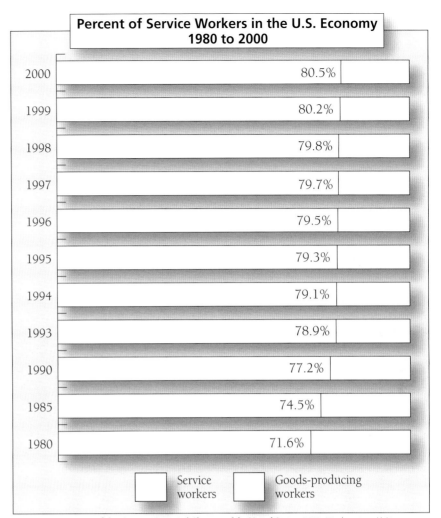

Source. U.S. Bureau of the Census, *Statistical Abstracts of the United States*, 2001, Washington, D.C., Government Printing Office, http://www.census.gov/prod/2002pubs/01statab/labor.pdf (March 26, 2003).

in a service economy has a different role from the consumer in a manufacturing economy. A person buying a refrigerator has only to pay for it for the transaction to be a success, but a person visiting a doctor has to tell the doctor all sorts of things, for example, what hurts, personal and family medical histories, and must constantly respond for the medical visit to be a success.

Labor in the Service Economy

Services are difficult to define partly because the service sector is far from homogenous. Service jobs encompass low-paying jobs, for example, waiting on tables and answering phones, as well as high-paying professions, for example, doctors, lawyers, consultants, or investment bankers.

The service sector is usually broken down into smaller sectors. One sector that

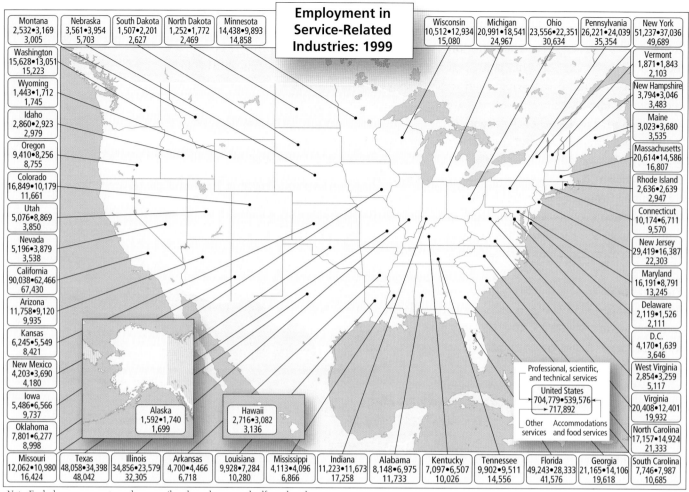

Employment in Service-Related Industries: 1999

State	Professional, scientific, and technical services • Other services	Accommodations and food services
Montana	2,532 • 3,169	3,005
Nebraska	3,561 • 3,954	5,703
South Dakota	1,507 • 2,201	2,627
North Dakota	1,252 • 1,772	2,469
Minnesota	14,438 • 9,893	14,858
Wisconsin	10,512 • 12,934	15,080
Michigan	20,991 • 18,541	24,967
Ohio	23,556 • 22,351	30,634
Pennsylvania	26,221 • 24,039	35,354
New York	51,237 • 37,036	49,689
Washington	15,628 • 13,051	15,223
Wyoming	1,443 • 1,712	1,745
Idaho	2,860 • 2,923	2,979
Oregon	9,410 • 8,256	8,755
Colorado	16,849 • 10,179	11,661
Utah	5,076 • 8,869	3,850
Nevada	5,196 • 3,879	3,538
California	90,038 • 62,466	67,430
Arizona	11,758 • 9,120	9,935
Kansas	6,245 • 5,549	8,421
New Mexico	4,203 • 3,690	4,180
Iowa	5,486 • 6,566	9,737
Oklahoma	7,801 • 6,277	8,998
Vermont	1,871 • 1,843	2,103
New Hampshire	3,794 • 3,046	3,483
Maine	3,023 • 3,680	3,535
Massachusetts	20,614 • 14,586	16,807
Rhode Island	2,636 • 2,639	2,947
Connecticut	10,174 • 6,711	9,570
New Jersey	29,419 • 16,387	22,303
Maryland	16,191 • 8,791	13,245
Delaware	2,119 • 1,526	2,111
D.C.	4,170 • 1,639	3,646
West Virginia	2,854 • 3,259	5,117
Virginia	20,408 • 12,401	19,932
North Carolina	17,157 • 14,924	21,333
Alaska	1,592 • 1,740	1,699
Hawaii	2,716 • 3,082	3,136
Missouri	12,062 • 10,980	16,424
Texas	48,058 • 34,398	48,042
Illinois	34,856 • 23,579	32,305
Arkansas	4,700 • 4,466	6,718
Louisiana	9,928 • 7,284	10,280
Mississippi	4,113 • 4,096	6,866
Indiana	11,223 • 11,673	17,258
Alabama	8,148 • 6,975	11,733
Kentucky	7,097 • 6,507	10,026
Tennessee	9,902 • 9,511	14,556
Florida	49,243 • 28,333	41,576
Georgia	21,165 • 14,106	19,618
South Carolina	7,746 • 7,987	10,685

Professional, scientific, and technical services
United States 704,779 • 539,576 → 717,892
Other services   Accommodations and food services

Note: Excludes government employees, railroad employees, and self-employed persons.
Source: U.S. Bureau of the Census, *County Business Patterns*, Washington, D.C., Government Printing Office, 2000.

became considerably larger in the 1960s and 1970s was government jobs. Because government is essentially a service for its citizens and does not produce material goods, it is considered part of the service sector. Education and health care are also considered part of the service sector.

Consumer services include jobs in retail, restaurants, and hair salons. Consumer service jobs tend to pay low wages; they also tend to require little education. Although these jobs might be the stereotypical form of service sector employment, in reality the percentage of people employed in consumer services has declined over the past several decades, mainly because of decreasing employment of maids and other household servants.

In economic terms, services are labor intensive, not capital intensive like manufacturing. A manufacturer relies largely on equipment and machinery—capital—to perform; a service business relies on its people. Indeed, some service businesses acknowledge this by referring to their employees as "human capital."

The relational aspect of services also makes the individual service provider a very important figure. For example, a doctor must spend years in school and get special accreditation before she may practice medicine. Even so, she might not be a good doctor, and society considers her performance to be so important that she can be sued or even imprisoned for not doing her job correctly.

The labor-intensive aspect of services led to speculation that services could not take advantage of economies of scale (the lower costs of making things that often result from making more of them). For instance, a doctor is only one person and can see only a certain number of patients a day.

However, during the 1990s service industries did appear to be able to organize around economies of scale. The consulting industry, for example, became increasingly dominated by large firms, which had the effect of spreading administrative costs over a larger group of employees. The rise of that industry in itself also suggested economies of scale at work: a group of people with extremely specialized knowledge who set up a consulting firm then apply that knowledge to several different companies concurrently—thus the specialized knowledge is applied to more places for less cost.

Producer Services

An increasingly important part of the service sector is producer services, or services sold to businesses. This sector includes finance, insurance, real estate, legal services, consulting,

and so on. Producer services have grown as businesses have become larger, more international, and more complex. A business interested in starting operations abroad, for example, will probably employ a number of producer-service professionals to determine where to locate the operation, to help it navigate unfamiliar laws and regulations, and to finance the venture. The business may hire those workers from outside, or it may have in-house departments dedicated to various kinds of producer services.

Producer services have also grown because of changes in manufacturer operations. Ironically, one of the reasons that the manufacturing economy has declined is greater hiring from the service sector by manufacturers. Manufacturers have become increasingly reliant on technology and automation, which changes the kind of

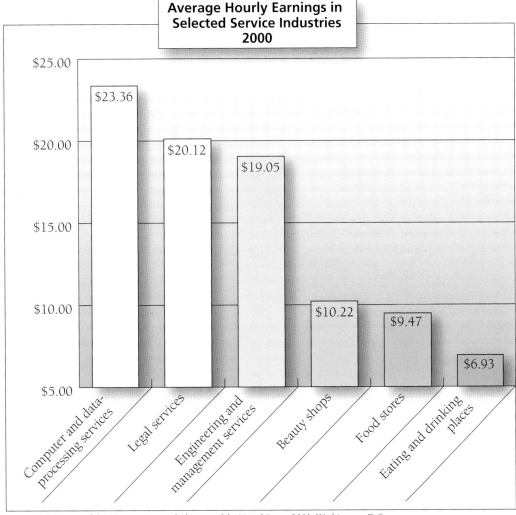

Average Hourly Earnings in Selected Service Industries 2000

- Computer and data-processing services: $23.36
- Legal services: $20.12
- Engineering and management services: $19.05
- Beauty shops: $10.22
- Food stores: $9.47
- Eating and drinking places: $6.93

Source: U.S. Bureau of the Census, *Statistical Abstracts of the United States,* 2001, Washington, D.C., Government Printing Office, 2002.

worker they tend to hire. A manufacturer can install an automated assembly line, with robots networked to a computer monitor that displays their status. Instead of hundreds of manufacturing-sector workers, the manufacturer needs only a handful—plus many service-sector workers to service the robots, design the networking software, and address computer problems.

If producer services blur the line between the manufacturing and service sectors, they can also blur the line between goods and services. Purchase a computer assembled by those in the manufacturing sector and it comes with software created by those in the service sector. It also may come with a service contract, which requires service-sector employees to fulfill.

Salaries for service workers vary widely depending on the service. Computer consultants are some of the best-paid service workers.

Blurring the line between selling services and selling goods has always been the norm in restaurants but is increasingly becoming the norm in other fields as well because services add value to goods, giving them a competitive edge in the marketplace. Most consumers would rather buy a computer that comes with software and a service contract rather than a computer that needs basic software installed.

As a result, economists are increasingly viewing the service sector as a complement to manufacturing and a benefit to the national economy. In a service economy, goods and manufacturing do not disappear because many of the services revolve around them. Instead, goods and manufacturing are bolstered by services—goods are more competitive, manufacturing companies are more profitable, and workers are more productive.

Of course, adjustments by workers are required. If, as seems likely, manufacturing industries employ more and more service-sector workers, the old-fashioned manufacturing job, which paid fairly well and demanded more physical strength and endurance than education, is going to become even more endangered.

Service-sector jobs, in contrast, tend to either pay quite well or pay poorly; the determining factor is usually education and training rather than size and strength. Indeed, the gap in wages and employment is growing between workers with a college education and those without. Workers, especially women, have responded by seeking more education. From 1982 to 2000 the percentage of American workers with some college education rose from 33 percent to 51 percent.

The late 1990s were a time of high growth and increasing productivity that seemed to put to rest some of the earlier concerns about the service economy. Clearly, manufacturing will not disappear and goods will continue to matter, even as the service sector remains dominant. As economists continue in their attempts to understand the service economy, more optimistic assessments are coming to the

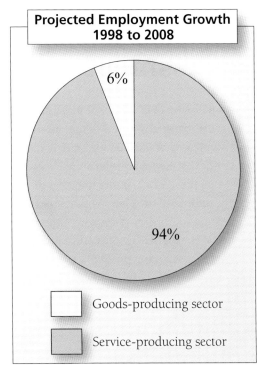

Projected Employment Growth 1998 to 2008

6%

94%

☐ Goods-producing sector

▨ Service-producing sector

Source: Bureau of Labor Statistics, "Service Sector Dominant Source of New Jobs," *MLR: The Editor's Desk*, 1999, http://www.bls.gov/opub/ted/1999/Nov/wk5/art05.txt (March 26, 2003).

fore: services may be less vulnerable to recession and allow American products to compete globally. Current understanding of the service economy may not be any more accurate than past assessments, but as services seem here to stay, ample opportunity will be available to find out.

Further Reading

Blair, Margaret M., and Steven M. H. Wallman. *Unseen Wealth: Report of the Brookings Task Force on Intangibles.* Washington, D.C.: Brookings Institution Press, 2001.

Fuchs, Victor R. *The Service Economy.* New York: National Bureau of Economic Research, 1968.

Illeris, Sven. *The Service Economy: A Geographical Approach.* New York: John Wiley & Sons, 1996.

Riddle, Dorothy I. *Service-Led Growth: The Role of the Service Sector in World Development.* New York: Praeger, 1986.

Shelp, Ronald Kent. *Beyond Industrialization: Ascendancy of the Global Service Economy.* New York: Praeger, 1981.

Stanback, Thomas M., Jr., et al. *Services: The New Economy.* Totowa, N.J.: Allanheld, Osmun, 1981.

—*Mary Sisson*

See also:
Civil Rights Legislation; Equal Employment Opportunity Commission; Women in the Workforce; Working Conditions.

Sexual Harassment

Sexual harassment is a form of sex discrimination involving unwanted sexual attention that humiliates or intimidates and is based on gender or sexual preference. Women constitute the overwhelming majority of targets; according to the National Organization for Women, studies suggest that most women will experience some form of sexual harassment at some point in their lives. Although women are more likely to be subjected to sexual harassment, men also can be victims. Further, a harasser may be of the same or the opposite gender as the victim.

Sexual harassment in the United States is considered a violation of the victim's civil rights. Among the activities that may be considered harassment are suggestive comments about one's appearance; touching or other physical contact; sexual comments or jokes; exposure to sexually explicit material; and sexual advances. In addition, even if the harassment is not directed at a particular person, it may create an environment that is hostile to that person's ability to function, which is also considered harassment.

Sexual Harassment and the Law

In 1964 Congress enacted Title VII of the Civil Rights Act, which prohibited an employer from discriminating against an individual with respect to compensation, terms, conditions, or privileges of employment because of, among other factors, the individual's sex. In 1980 the Equal Employment Opportunity Commission (EEOC), the federal agency responsible for administering Title VII, issued guidelines specifying that sexual harassment, as therein defined, was a form of sex discrimination prohibited by Title VII. However, not until 1986, 22 years later, did the U.S. Supreme Court first address the issue of sexual harassment in *Meritor Savings Bank, FSB v. Vinson*. The Court ruled that discrimination on the basis of sex included sexual harassment. Precisely what constitutes sexual harassment and how to regulate it have since been the subject of considerable litigation and controversy under federal, state, and local laws.

Defining Sexual Harassment

Sexual Misconduct
- Unwelcome advances
- Requests for favors
- Other verbal or physical conduct of a sexual nature

plus

Quid Pro Quo
- Submission to or rejection of unwelcome sexual conduct is basis for employment decisions
- Involves manager or supervisor
- Requires tangible action: discharge, demotion, or failure to promote

or

Hostile Environment
- Conduct, the purpose or effect of which interferes with work performance
- Conduct creating intimidating, hostile, or offensive environment
- May involve non-managerial coworkers or third parties

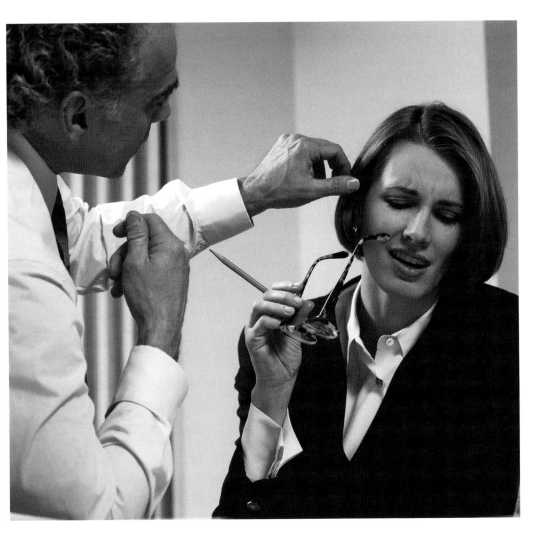

Unwelcome physical contact by a colleague can be sexual harassment.

Two distinct forms of sexual harassment have been identified: quid pro quo and hostile work environment. Quid pro quo is the more easily defined. In the words of the EEOC, it occurs when an employee's "submission to or rejection of unwelcome sexual conduct . . . is used as a basis for employment decisions." By definition, it necessarily involves behavior by a manager or supervisor and requires some tangible employment action—discharge, demotion, or failure to promote.

Hostile work environment, the kind of harassment that has triggered the most litigation and controversy, involves unwelcome sexual conduct that has the purpose or effect of unreasonably interfering with an employee's work performance or creating an intimidating, hostile, or offensive work environment. Unlike quid pro quo harassment, this kind of harassment also may involve conduct by nonmanagerial or nonsupervisory coworkers or third parties, for example, customers, vendors, or suppliers.

In *Meritor Savings Bank*, the Supreme Court made clear that Title VII prohibits both quid pro quo and hostile work environment harassment. In that and subsequent cases, however, the Supreme Court stressed that a hostile work environment generally will not be found where the conduct is isolated, innocuous, or simply offensive; rather, the harassment must be sufficiently severe or pervasive so as to alter the conditions of the victim's employment and create an abusive working relationship. At the same time, the Court has stated, establishing a claim of hostile work environment does not require conduct that seriously affects the employee's well-being or is physically or psychologically injurious.

In their *Faragher* and *Ellerth* decisions of 1998, the Supreme Court made clear that where the conduct is committed by a manager or supervisor, and the employee has suffered

David Papa of Deltona, Florida, holds a copy of a judgment awarding him $237,000 in November 1995—the first time the EEOC ruled for a male against a female in a sexual harassment case. Papa sued Domino's Pizza for sexual harassment after being fired by his female boss.

a "tangible adverse employment" action such as discharge, demotion, or a failure to promote, the employer will be held strictly liable, even though it was unaware of the conduct and the manager or supervisor was acting outside the scope of his or her authority. Absent any tangible employment action, the Court ruled, the employer still will be liable for the acts of a supervisor, unless it can affirmatively establish: (1) it exercised reasonable care to prevent and correct promptly any sexually harassing behavior, and (2) the employee unreasonably failed to take advantage of any preventive or corrective opportunities provided by the employer or to avoid harm otherwise.

In light of these possible defenses, an employer must establish, disseminate, and enforce a clear policy against sexual harassment, one that includes a viable complaint procedure. If employees, though aware of the policy and complaint procedure, fail to report the incidents or otherwise avail themselves of the complaint procedure, their claims, in the absence of a tangible employment action, might be deemed defective.

The need to regulate sexual harassment in the workplace is, by now, well accepted. The difficulties lie in the attempt to define what adult human behavior is prohibited and what is not; what is severe and pervasive, as opposed to offensive but innocuous or isolated. At what point does a misunderstanding or miscommunication between adults become actionable? Where do banter and horseplay end and harassing acts begin? To what extent do we assess the behavior in question in the context of our social mores? Are there issues of free speech? These are but a few of the workplace issues our courts, and society, are attempting to address.

Further Reading

Bouchard, Elizabeth. *Everything You Need to Know about Sexual Harassment.* New York: Rosen Publishing Group, 2001.

Crouch, Margaret A. *Thinking about Sexual Harassment: A Guide for the Perplexed.* New York: Oxford University Press, 2001.

Stein, Laura W. *Sexual Harassment in America: A Documentary History.* Westport, Conn.: Greenwood Press, 1999.

—*Michael I. Bernstein and Jo Lynn Southard*

Sherman Antitrust Act

As American businesses grew in size and strength, and, in some cases, gained market dominance during the latter half of the nineteenth century, opposition to monopolies took root as a political issue at both the federal and state levels. In 1890 the growth of corporate power prompted Congress to enact the Sherman Antitrust Act, which was the first federal law in this field. Antitrust law is aimed at the preservation of market competition and the restriction of anticompetitive economic behavior.

U.S. antitrust law has adapted to changes in social and economic conditions, for example, the urbanization of the population, rapid changes in technology, the advent of mass merchandising, and the globalization of business. Developments in antitrust policy have also been affected by changes in prevailing economic philosophy and membership of the judiciary.

Enforcement of the Sherman Act and other antitrust laws has varied depending on prevailing political, social, and economic views. The pendulum has swung from the active enforcement of the trust-busters at the start of the twentieth century to little enforcement during the Depression and World War II. In the late 1950s and in the 1960s Sherman Act prosecutions increased and, for the first time, corporate executives were sent to prison, a practice sometimes followed today. For example, a 2000 investigation of antitrust violations in the vitamin industry resulted in jail time for four former executives. The election of Ronald Reagan to the presidency in 1980 began a reduction in Sherman Act enforcement. In the latter half of the 1990s, with President Bill Clinton in the White House, Sherman Act prosecutions increased, with the Justice Department bringing suit against Microsoft and Intel.

Restraints of Trade

The Sherman Antitrust Act contains two main provisions. Section 1 outlaws contracts, combinations, or conspiracies in restraint of trade. Section 2 prohibits monopolies and attempts to monopolize. Both of these provisions were written in broad terms, leaving the courts wide latitude for interpretation. Such wide latitude gives the law the ability to adapt to future changes in technology and market conditions. During the last century, court decisions have generated a body of antitrust laws.

Section 1 provides that "[e]very contract, combination in the form of trust or otherwise, or conspiracy, in restraint of trade or commerce among the several states or with foreign nations is hereby declared to be

See also:
Cartel; Competition; Federal Trade Commission; Monopoly; Regulation of Business and Industry.

Lawmaker John Sherman in an undated daguerreotype.

WHEN McKINLEY IS PRESIDENT. *1896*

A political cartoon from 1896 shows Uncle Sam shut out of the White House while monopolies are welcomed inside.

illegal." Taken literally, this language is so broad that every contract could be deemed to be a restraint of trade. To avoid such an impractical arrangement, courts have interpreted Section 1 to prohibit only unreasonable restraints of trade (or those that harm competition among businesses). Examples of the use of Section 1 to stop unreasonable restraints of trade are the breakups of Standard Oil in 1911 and AT&T in 1984. Ultimately, AT&T was divided into a new AT&T and several "baby Bells" or regional phone companies.

Many elements must be present to establish a violation of Section 1. A prosecutor or private plaintiff must prove all of the following for a violation of Section 1 to exist: (1) an agreement must exist; (2) between two or more parties; (3) that unreasonably restrains trade or competition; (4) in or affecting interstate commerce. Also, in a civil action, the agreement must have damaged the private plaintiff in his or her business or property. In a criminal antitrust case, the defendant must be shown to have acted with criminal intent.

Agreements that violate Section 1 can be either horizontal or vertical. A horizontal restraint involves collaboration or collusion among competitors at the same level in the economic process. For example, an agreement among manufacturers, wholesalers, or retailers would be horizontal. An agreement made by parties that are not in direct competition at the same level is a vertical restraint; an agreement between a manufacturer and a wholesaler is vertical. Typically, horizontal agreements are illegal per se (in and of themselves) whereas vertical agreements are analyzed using the "rule of reason" test, which is essentially a rule of common sense.

Over time, the U.S. Supreme Court divided unreasonable or illegal restraints into two categories. One category includes practices deemed illegal per se. Such illegal practices include price fixing; fixing other terms of sale, for example, discounts, advertising allowances, credit terms, or warranty provisions; agreements to restrict production; allocation of markets; and certain refusals to deal. The second category includes other forms of restraint, which are judged under the rule of reason. This standard requires that courts, in deciding whether a challenged business practice unreasonably restricts competition, consider such factors as the makeup of the industry involved, the defendant company's position within the industry, the ability of competitors to respond to the challenged practice, and the defendant firm's reason for adopting the practice.

The statute also requires that the trade restrained must either be in or at least have an effect on interstate commerce. Historically, the standard for establishing this element has not been especially stringent. The U.S. Supreme Court has indicated that showing that the challenged activity has a not-insubstantial effect on the interstate commerce involved is sufficient.

Monopolies

Economic analysis demonstrates that a monopoly will use its power to limit production and increase prices. Section 2 of the Sherman Act outlaws both agreements among businesses and conduct by one firm. Courts have delineated two requirements for a claim for monopolization to be upheld: (1) possession of monopoly or market power in a relevant market and (2) willful acquisition and maintenance of that power through improper means (in contrast to having acquired and maintained monopoly power through creation of a superior product or service or business acumen).

Monopoly or market power is the ability to control prices or to exclude competitors from the relevant market. Exclusion of competition has two elements: a product (the "product market") and a location (the "geographic market"). Definition of the relevant market is significant. Usually, the broader the market, the less likely a firm being sued will be found to have monopoly power.

A claim of monopolization also requires proof that the accused monopolist obtained or maintained its monopoly through unfair or predatory conduct. The courts have yet to agree on what constitutes such conduct. To make such determination, the federal courts must balance the conflict between the fear of monopolies and the policy of encouraging successful competition that leads to market power. One example of predatory conduct is predatory pricing and price squeezes like those of the 1945 *Alcoa* case in which Alcoa was found to have overcharged competing aluminum ingot processors so that they could not successfully compete. Another kind of predatory conduct is refusal to allow competitors to use facilities essential for effective competition, for example, the 1912 *Terminal Railroad Association* case in which several railroad companies formed a group to deny nonmember rail firms the use of terminals. Other examples include misuse of product information to gain a competitive advantage and customer restrictions to exclude competition.

The Sherman Antitrust Act
(Excerpt)

Sec. 1. Every contract, combination in the form of trust or otherwise; or conspiracy, in restraint of trade or commerce among the several States, or with foreign nations, is hereby declared to be illegal. Every person who shall make any such contract or engage in any such combination or conspiracy, shall be deemed guilty of a misdemeanor, and, on conviction thereof, shall be punished by fine not exceeding five thousand dollars, or by imprisonment not exceeding one year, or by both said punishments, in the discretion of the court.

Sec. 2. Every person who shall monopolize, or attempt to monopolize, or combine or conspire with any other person or persons, to monopolize any part of the trade or commerce among the several States, or with foreign nations, shall be deemed guilty of a misdemeanor, and, on conviction thereof, shall be punished by fine not exceeding five thousand dollars, or by imprisonment not exceeding one year, or by both said punishments, in the discretion of the court.

Sec. 3. Every contract, combination in form of trust or otherwise, or conspiracy, in restraint of trade or commerce in any Territory of the United States or of the District of Columbia, or in restraint of trade or commerce between any such Territory and another, or between any such Territory or Territories and any State or States or the District of Columbia, or with foreign nations, or between the District of Columbia and any States or States or foreign nations, is hereby declared illegal. Every person who shall make any such contract or engage in any such combination or conspiracy, shall be deemed guilty of a misdemeanor, and, on conviction thereof, shall be punished by fine not exceeding five thousand dollars, or by imprisonment not exceeding one year, or by both said punishments, in the discretion of the court.

Section 2 also outlaws attempts to monopolize. An example is the government's lawsuit against Microsoft. The standard test applied by courts requires proof of a specific intent to monopolize plus a reasonable probability of success. Recent cases, including the 1985 case in which the Aspen Skiing Company refused to continue a joint marketing program with a smaller competitor, indicate that the greater the measure of market power a firm possesses, the less flagrant must be its conduct to constitute an attempt to monopolize.

The language of the Sherman Act is simple and general. The law's scope is limited only by the common sense and the logic of the judges who interpret it. Case law surrounding the Sherman Act continues to evolve as new decisions are rendered. Hence, the courts have the flexibility to respond to changing market conditions and new economic ideas about the workings of competitive markets that may emerge in the twenty-first century. Antitrust laws, including the Sherman Act, have adapted to new circumstances through establishment of guidelines relating specific industries with definitions of lawful conduct. The question remains, however, whether the courts can make antitrust decisions in a timely enough manner to be truly responsive to changing markets and technological developments.

Further Reading

Aarts, Jack W. *Antitrust Policy Versus Economic Power.* Leiden, Netherlands: Stenfert Kroese, 1975.

Agnew, J. H. *Competition Law.* London: Allen & Unwin, 1985.

Areeda, P. E., and H. Hovenkamp. *Antitrust Law: An Analysis of Antitrust Principles and Their Application.* Gaithersburg, Md.: Aspen Publishers, 2002.

Bork, Robert H. *Antitrust Paradox: A Policy at War with Itself.* New York: Free Press, 1993.

Hobbs, Casswell O., and Robert Schlossberg. *Antitrust Strategies for Mergers, Acquisitions, Joint Ventures, and Strategic Alliances.* Newark, N.J.: Lexis Nexis Matthew Bender, 2000.

—*Carl Pacini*

Sikorsky, Igor

1889–1972
Aviation pioneer

Igor Sikorsky began designing helicopters even before the first airplanes had been created. Sikorsky's first helicopter, built when he was 12 years old, was a model powered by rubber bands and inspired by the drawings of Leonardo da Vinci and the stories of Jules Verne.

Igor Ivanovich Sikorsky was born in Kiev, the Ukraine, on May 25, 1889. His parents, Ivan and Zinaida Sikorsky, were both doctors. Sikorsky entered the Russian naval academy in Saint Petersburg in 1903 but left in 1906 to study engineering in Paris. In 1909 Sikorsky returned to Kiev with a three-cylinder 25-horsepower Anzani motorcycle engine and built a helicopter with coaxial twin-bladed rotors. The crude machine used wires, pulled by the pilot, to change the pitch of the blades. Sikorsky was able to demonstrate rotary-wing lift, but the finished helicopter was never able to lift its own weight. Sikorsky returned to Paris that year to study airplane design instead.

Airplane Engineer

During the next three years Sikorsky experimented with designs for airplanes. His sixth plane, the S-6, received the highest award at the 1912 Moscow Aviation Exhibition and first prize in a military competition at Saint Petersburg.

The success of the S-6 led to a position as chief engineer of the aviation subsidiary of the Russian Baltic Railroad Car Works. In the Baltics, 14 single-engine planes suffered from engine failure caused by mosquito-clogged carburetors. To solve the problem, Sikorsky invented the multiengine plane. Completed in 1913, the world's first multiengine airplane was called *The Grand*. The four-engine aircraft had an 89-foot wingspan and featured a bathroom, upholstered chairs,

See also:
Defense Industry;
Trippe, Juan.

Igor Sikorsky working with an airplane model, circa 1950s.

and an exterior catwalk on top of the fuselage where passengers could take a walk in the air.

The success of *The Grand* led to the building of the bigger S-22 the following year (named the *Ilya Muromets*, after a tenth-century Russian hero). More than 70 military versions of the S-22 were built for use as bombers by the Imperial Russian Air Force during World War I.

The Russian Revolution of 1917 drove Sikorsky from his position in Russian aviation. He went to France, where he was commissioned to build a bomber for Allied service, but the aircraft was still on the drawing board when World War I ended. Unable to find another position in France, Sikorsky immigrated to the United States in March 1919. For a time Sikorsky taught mathematics to fellow émigrés on New York's Lower East Side.

Sikorsky Manufacturing Corporation and the Flying Boats

Finally, in 1923, a group of students and friends who knew of Sikorsky's reputation in prewar Russia pooled their resources and launched the Sikorsky Aero Engineering Corporation. The company started production on a farm near Roosevelt Field, Long Island, New York, using army surplus materials and parts from junkyards. Sikorsky's first plane for his own company was the S-29A (A for America), which first flew in September 1924. The S-29A was a twin-engine, all-metal transport and would prove to be the forerunner of the modern airplane. In 1925 the company was renamed the Sikorsky Manufacturing Corporation.

Sikorsky experimented with a number of twin-engine aircraft, but the company achieved its greatest success to date in 1928 with the nine-seat S-38 amphibian. The S-38 was the plane used by Pan American Airways to pioneer routes to and in Central and South America. The S-38 was eventually used by 10 airlines and the U.S. Navy. Sikorsky's company also designed and built the famous Flying Clippers that pioneered commercial air transportation across both the Atlantic and Pacific Oceans. Again, Pan American Airways used the Clippers to popularize long-distance air travel and make it a possibility for millions of average people.

Return to the Helicopter

With the success of his company, Sikorsky returned to his childhood dream—helicopters. In 1931 he had patented a design with the now-familiar helicopter layout—a single large main rotor and a small anti-torque tail rotor. Sikorsky designed the steel tube, open cockpit VS-300 and flew it for the first time on September 14, 1939. (Sikorsky always insisted that he pilot the first flight of a new aircraft.) By the summer of 1940 the experimental helicopter could stay airborne for 15 minutes.

The VS-300 would crash several times and undergo major changes during years of test flying, but by 1943 Sikorsky was able to achieve large-scale manufacture of the R-4,

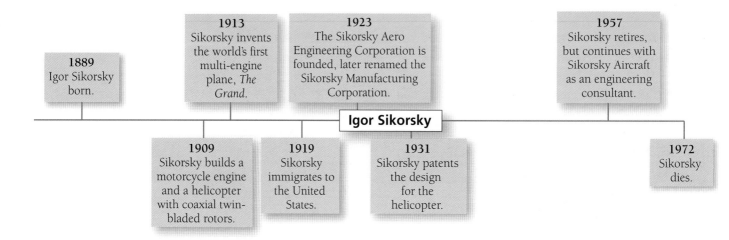

1889 Igor Sikorsky born.

1909 Sikorsky builds a motorcycle engine and a helicopter with coaxial twin-bladed rotors.

1913 Sikorsky invents the world's first multi-engine plane, *The Grand*.

1919 Sikorsky immigrates to the United States.

1923 The Sikorsky Aero Engineering Corporation is founded, later renamed the Sikorsky Manufacturing Corporation.

Igor Sikorsky

1931 Sikorsky patents the design for the helicopter.

1957 Sikorsky retires, but continues with Sikorsky Aircraft as an engineering consultant.

1972 Sikorsky dies.

the world's first production helicopter, built for the U.S. military. Sikorsky had not anticipated the helicopter's popularity on military missions, but he was especially proud of the helicopter's use in rescue work. A Sikorsky R-4 flew the first helicopter mercy mission through a snowstorm in January 1944, hauling blood plasma from Battery Park in Lower Manhattan to Sandy Hook, New Jersey, to aid victims of a steamship explosion. In November 1945 an S-51 conducted the first helicopter hoist rescue when it pulled two seamen from a sinking barge off Connecticut. In World War II fabric-covered Sikorsky helicopters flew the first combat rescue and Medevac missions.

Today, Sikorsky Aircraft Corporation is a subsidiary of Connecticut-based United Technologies Corporation and is still a world leader in the design and manufacture of advanced helicopters. Sikorsky helicopters are used by all five branches of the U.S. military and by military services and commercial operators in more than 40 countries. Revenues in 2000 were $1.8 billion.

The Sikorsky Aircraft Corporation has designed and built the armed reconnaissance helicopter RAH-66 Comanche and the famous S-70 Black Hawk, which has been sold to more than 25 governments. Sikorsky helicopters are also famous for their use in executive transport, offshore oil exploration, search and rescue, and emergency medical service missions.

Although he retired in 1957, at the age of 68, Sikorsky continued to work as an engineering consultant for Sikorsky Aircraft and was at his desk the day before he died, on October 26, 1972, at the age of 83. The awards and honors given to Sikorsky during his lifetime would fill many pages. They include the National Medal of Science, the Wright Brothers Memorial Trophy, the U.S. Air Force Academy's Thomas D. White National Defense Award, and the Royal Aeronautical Society of England's Silver Medal. He is honored at both the International Aerospace and the Aviation Halls of Fame.

The Sikorsky CH-53E over Arizona in 1996.

Further Reading

Capelotti, P. J. *Explorer's Air Yacht: The Sikorsky S-38 Flying Boat.* Missoula, Mont.: Pictorial Histories Publishing, 1995.

Delear, Frank J. *Igor Sikorsky: His Three Careers in Aviation.* New York: Dodd, Mead, 1976.

Hunt, William E. *"Heelicopter": Pioneering with Igor Sikorsky.* Shrewsbury, U.K.: Airlife Pub., 1998.

Pember, Harry E. *Sikorsky VS-44 Flying Boat.* Boulder, Colo.: Flying Machines Press, 1998.

Spenser, Jay P. *Whirlybirds: A History of the U.S. Helicopter Pioneers.* Seattle: University of Washington Press, 1998.

—*Lisa Magloff*

Silent Spring

In 1962 Rachel Carson, a marine biologist and author, published a gripping account of the environmental harm caused by pesticides. The book, *Silent Spring*, indicted the U.S. government for understating the toxic impact of insecticides like DDT and implicated the chemical industry and agribusinesses in production and use of biohazardous materials. *Silent Spring* significantly raised public awareness of pollution as a health problem, leading to state and federal regulation of toxins and ongoing attention to the relationship between modern technologies and nature.

Carson was uniquely qualified to educate others about the environmental impact of toxic chemicals. Born in 1907 in Springdale, Pennsylvania, she earned a bachelor's degree in biology from the Pennsylvania College for Women in 1929 and a master's degree in zoology at John Hopkins University in 1932. Although women were not encouraged in science at that time, Carson maintained an unwavering commitment to the study of biology and oceanography. After the death of Carson's father and an older sister in the 1930s, Carson's income became the sole means of support for her mother and her sister's two children.

Carson began to focus on oceanography and the complex ecosystems of shorelines in 1929 when she worked at the renowned Woods Hole Marine Biological Laboratory on the coast of Massachusetts. In 1935 she was hired by the Federal Bureau of Fisheries in the Commerce Department and was promoted to junior aquatic biologist the following year. The bureau merged with the U.S. Biological Survey in 1939 to become the U.S. Fish and Wildlife Service (FWS).

Carson's work for the FWS included writing; by 1949 she had become editor of all FWS publications. In 1951 she published *The Sea Around Us*, a lyrical and scientifically accurate explanation of marine biology. It became a best-seller, prompting rerelease of her first book, *Under the Sea-Wind* (which had sold poorly upon initial publication in 1941). Carson retired in 1952 to devote herself to research and writing.

In her first two books and a third on oceanography, *The Edge of the Sea* (1955), Carson combined abundant scientific evidence with evocative images. Other scientists would do much more to develop the field studies and laboratory analyses that undergirded *Silent Spring,* but Carson's

---

Silent Spring
(Excerpt)

The figure is staggering and its implications are not easily grasped—500 new chemicals to which the bodies of men and animals are required somehow to adapt each year, chemicals totally outside the limits of biologic experience.

Among them are many that are used in man's war against nature. Since the mid-1940's over 200 basic chemicals have been created for use in killing insects, weeds, rodents, and other organisms described in the modern vernacular as "pests"; and they are sold under several thousand different brand names.

These sprays, dusts, and aerosols are now applied almost universally to farms, gardens, forests, and homes—nonselective chemicals that have the power to kill every insect, the "good" and the "bad," to still the song of birds and the leaping of fish in the streams, to coat the leaves with a deadly film, and to linger in the soil—all this though the intended target may be only a few weeds or insects. Can anyone believe it is possible to lay down such a barrage of poisons on the surface of the earth without making it unfit for all life? They should not be called insecticides, but "biocides."

—Rachel Carson, *Silent Spring*, 1962

skillful writing made such studies available for public education.

Many scientists had grown disturbed by the heavy use of chemical poisons common in the 1950s. World War II spurred growth in chemical research and development, and the chemical industries and agribusinesses profited from the amazing effectiveness of pesticides and insectides that could swiftly eradicate mosquitoes, ants, gypsy moths, and other pests. However, these synthetic toxins killed species other than their intended targets, and the toxins remained in the environment for years, eventually reaching humans through the food chain. The government agency that monitored pesticides, the Agricultural Research Service (ARS), had minimized the extent of the problem, and Carson wrote *Silent Spring* partly to debunk misleading arguments given in ARS and industrial publications and promotions.

Carson died in 1964, but the impact of *Silent Spring* continued to grow. President John F. Kennedy asked his Science Advisory Committee to investigate the book's claims, and its report affirmed *Silent Spring* while criticizing the U.S. Department of Agriculture, the Food and Drug Administration, chemical industries, and agribusiness. Under pressure from a worried public (reinforced by a CBS documentary on *Silent Spring* in 1963), members of Congress also investigated synthetic toxins. From the 1960s onward, conservation groups like the Audubon Society successfully lobbied state and federal legislatures for more regulation of toxic chemicals.

Agitation provoked by *Silent Spring* became a major force in the modern environmental movement, marked by the first celebration of Earth Day in 1970. Concern about chemical toxins has become a global issue, as some countries have resisted regulating substances banned in the United States, and toxins can cross borders through the international agriculture industry. Production of bio-friendly materials has expanded as entrepreneurs have responded to *Silent Spring* by developing less toxic forms of pest control. Legislatures and regulatory

Rachel Carson in an undated photograph.

agencies come under continuing pressure to monitor industrial and agricultural uses of chemicals, and industries face continuing pressure to decrease their use of toxic substances, thanks in part to the influence of *Silent Spring*.

Further Reading

Carson, Rachel. *Silent Spring.* 1962. Reprint, Boston: Houghton Mifflin, 2002.

Lear, Linda. "Bombshell in Beltsville: The USDA and the Challenge of 'Silent Spring'." *Agricultural History* 66 (Spring 1992): 151–170.

———. *Rachel Carson: Witness for Nature.* New York: Henry Holt, 1998.

Marco, Gino, Robert Hollingworth, and William Durham, eds. Silent Spring *Revisited.* Washington, D.C.: American Chemical Society, 1987.

—*Beth Kraig*

Small Business

The Small Business Administration Act defines a small business concern as a business that is independently owned and operated and is not dominant in its field of operation. For example, an agricultural enterprise is considered a small business if its annual receipts do not exceed $500,000. A study conducted by Joel Popkin and Company found that small businesses make up approximately 68 percent of services, 65 percent of wholesale and retail trade, and 27 percent of mining and manufacturing enterprises. Small business has continued to be an important part of the U.S. economy even through less stable times for larger businesses.

Brief History of Small Business

Before the Industrial Revolution, small business was the dominant form of economic enterprise in the United States. The production of textiles and food products as well as metal, wood, and leather goods was, in most cases, handled by small, family-based operations using local raw materials and serving their immediate communities. Scholars believe the early entrepreneurial spirit of small business owners helped create a recognizable business culture in America that continues to exist—a culture based on idealism, individualism, and the desire to be one's own boss.

The nineteenth century saw unprecedented growth in American small businesses, especially in the most common small business, the retail store. In 1814 the U.S. government issued more than 46,000 retail licenses (during the short time during which licensing was federally mandated). An additonal 12,000 retail stores were logged in the census of 1840, and that number grew to 720,000 by 1869. These general stores were often the hub of commerce during this era, especially in smaller towns. Meanwhile, peddlers—the quintessential one-person operation—traveled from town to town selling their wares. In 1850 more than 10,000 peddlers were on the road; by 1860, nearly 17,000. These general stores and peddlers carried out the distribution of goods and services in America well into the 1870s.

The grocery store of Fred Gower, in Baltimore, circa 1920.

In the 1870s the rail system in the United States opened up the local markets dominated by small business, allowing big business access for the first time. Advances in technology created economies of scale for larger companies, allowing for previously impossible efficiencies. Nevertheless, the number of smaller businesses continued to grow. They existed in the niches neglected by big business, for example, in local markets, producing specialized goods and often offering high levels of craftsmanship. Small businesses enabled skilled workers to survive in the face of unskilled assembly line work, and they provided service—in the old-fashioned sense of face-to-face contact and first-name-basis encounters. At this time, the absolute number of small businesses was growing as well. By the turn of the century, nearly two-thirds of all American workers were employed by small businesses.

As big business came to dominate the economic landscape, the federal government stepped in to help small businesses survive. America's first antitrust laws, the Sherman Act in 1890 and the Clayton Act in 1914, were passed mainly to protect small business. After nearly 110,000 businesses failed during the Great Depression, the government responded with the Robinson–Patman Act of 1936 (also known as the Anti-Chain-Store Act) and the Miller–Tydings Act of 1937 (also known as the Fair Trade Act), both of which sought to protect smaller retail firms from unfair pricing practices by national chain stores. After World War II, when small businesses found they could not compete with the large businesses that had dominated wartime production, the federal government stepped in once again, establishing the Small Business Administration (SBA) in 1953.

Scholarly interest in small business and small business history grew in the 1970s and 1980s, sparked, in part, by economic encroachment of foreign competition. Over the next several decades, most business schools and universities throughout the nation began to offer courses on developing and operating small businesses, and bookstore shelves began to fill with titles on

small business management. Contemporary small businesses continue to struggle to compete with large chain stores, but economists and entrepreneurs alike look to small businesses for innovation, flexible production, and specialization.

Starting a Small Business

The SBA offers major assistance in the starting of a small business. The SBA is the nation's largest single financial backer of small business. Before starting a small business, SBA recommends that entrepreneurs evaluate their personal and business goals, including completing a sound business plan. Before developing a plan, entrepreneurs should list the reasons that they are interested in starting a business and then

A shrimper and his staff outside his store in Bayou La Batre, Alabama.

ask themselves which kind of business would be right for them based on interests, skills, and time available to run the business. Prospective entrepreneurs may wish to evaluate themselves on such characteristics as stamina, level of organization, and the business's effect on their family.

In addition, a potential entrepreneur should conduct some research to determine market potential in the geographic area. Prospective business owners should try to identify competitors and plan the niche that their business will fill in the market. Profitable and competitive prices for services and goods are determined by analyzing production costs, including materials, labor, and overhead. Setting prices can be complicated, thus new business owners are advised to seek the advice of an expert.

A decision must be made about whether to start the business as a sole proprietorship (the easiest and least expensive method), to develop a partnership, or to incorporate. The structure of the business should take into consideration the kind of business operation, legal restrictions, liabilities, capital needs, number of employees, and tax

advantages. The SBA suggests that a tax accountant or attorney assist in making these decisions.

Prospective business owners should draw up a business plan. Included in the plan are a current and pro forma balance sheet, an income statement, and a cash flow analysis. Assistance in planning is available through SBA and also through the Service Corps of Retired Executives (SCORE) and Women's Business Centers (WBCs). In addition, resources are available through procurement center representatives at each major military installation and through more than 2,700 chambers of commerce located across the United States.

Once a plan is developed, information about licenses, zoning laws, and other regulations can be obtained through the local SBA or chamber of commerce. Entrepreneurs need to investigate the local, state, and federal governmental regulations that would apply to the business. For example, a certificate of occupancy will be needed if planning to occupy a new or used building. Businesses that use a name other than the owner's must register the name with the county according to the Trade Name Registration Act. State

Sarah of Sarah's Kitchen in Ruston, Louisiana, in the 1990s.

Estimates of Business Wealth by Firm Size
1990 to 2000
(in billions of dollars)

Year	Corporate wealth (small firms)	Corporate wealth (large firms)	Noncorporate wealth	Total business wealth	Total small business wealth	Small business share of corporate wealth (%)	Small business share of total business wealth (%)
1990	909	2,328	2,478	5,716	3,387	28.1	59.3
1992	1,764	3,214	2,404	7,381	4,168	35.4	56.5
1997	3,920	7,876	3,176	14,972	7,096	33.2	47.4
1998	3,751	10,026	3,508	17,285	7,259	27.2	42.0
1999	5,369	11,827	3,757	20,953	9,126	31.2	43.6
2000	4,288	11,108	4,039	19,434	8,327	27.9	42.8

Note: Market value of corporate wealth and new worth of noncorporate business.
Source: Small Business Administration, "Estimate of Business Wealth by Firm Size," *Small Business Research Summary,* September 2002.

and local government offices can provide more information about this regulation. Depending on the kind of business, owners may wish to investigate trademarks and copyrights, which can be registered through the state or federal government (U.S. Department of Commerce).

In estimating financing needs, a business owner should have enough money on hand to cover operating expenses for at least a year, after building and equipment expenses are covered. This includes the owner's salary and money to repay loans. An accountant can help estimate cash flow needs. In addition to committing personal funds, entrepreneurs may wish to consider a partner for additional financing. Banks are one source of financing; other sources include commercial finance companies, venture capital firms, local development companies, and life insurance companies.

Taxes should be taken into consideration when starting a new business. Business owners must contact the U.S. Internal Revenue Service (IRS) to obtain information about taxes that need to be withheld. Many publications are available from the IRS. The Social Security Administration can provide information on FICA. Information on sales tax and unemployment insurance tax can be obtained from the state government.

Other information must be gathered before starting a small business: benefits and state labor laws concerning employees should be investigated; health and safety standards can be obtained through the Federal Occupational Safety and Health Administration (OSHA). The U.S. Department of Labor provides information on minimum wage.

A successful business usually includes sound management practices, industry experience, technical support, and planning ability. The availability of many resources and the innovations of entrepreneurs enable small businesses to continue to be an important part of the business world.

Further Reading

Blackford, Mansel G. *A History of Small Business in America.* Chapel Hill: University of North Carolina Press, 2003.

Bruchey, Stuart W., ed. *Small Business in American Life.* New York: Columbia University Press, 1980.

Burton, E. James, and Steven M. Bragg. *Accounting and Finance for Your Small Business.* New York: John Wiley & Sons, 2001.

Panzarino, Frank. *Telecommunications Technologies for Small Business.* Upper Saddle River, N.J.: Prentice Hall PTR, 2002.

Stephenson, James. *Entrepreneur's Ultimate Start-up Directory.* Irvine, Calif.: Entrepreneur Press, 2001.

U.S. Department of Labor. *Crossing the Bridge to Self-Employment.* Washington, D.C.: Government Printing Office, 2001.

U.S. Small Business Administration. "The Facts about Small Business Development Centers." SBA No. FS-0043, November 2000.

—*Denise Davis and Laura Lambert*

See also:

Entrepreneurship; Small Business.

Small Business Administration

The Small Business Administration (SBA) is an independent federal agency designed to assist and promote the development of small business enterprises in the United States, as well as to help families recover from natural disasters. The SBA has four basic strategies for helping small businesses succeed: improve access to capital and credit; improve access to procurement opportunities; improve access to business development; and serve as a voice for small business. In addition, when natural disasters strike, the SBA offers special loans to families to help repair damage to their homes.

In 1953 President Dwight Eisenhower signed into law a bill passed by Congress authorizing the creation of the SBA. Its charter stated that "the Government should aid, counsel, assist, and protect . . . the interests of small-business concerns in order to preserve free competitive enterprise [and] to insure that a fair proportion of the total purchases and contracts or subcontracts for property and services for the Government . . . be placed with small-business enterprises." When Congress created the SBA, it did so with an eye on the past as well as to the future; by 1953 the federal government had already been assisting small business owners for nearly two decades.

The first direct assistance that the federal government provided to small business owners came from the Reconstruction Finance Corporation (RFC), which had been established to provide businesses large and small with loans during the Great Depression. For many businesses these loans were the difference between survival and collapse. In 1952, with the Depression over and the troops back home, Congress decided to eliminate the RFC. However, the lending program had proven so important for small business owners that it became the centerpiece of the new SBA. The new policies of the SBA ensured that the federal government would support small business owners for many years.

In addition to granting the SBA lending authority, Congress required the SBA to help small business owners with procurement. Procurement is the process whereby the government hires private companies to make products or perform services for it. The most common kinds of procurement needs are weapons and supplies for the military. When the United States entered World War II, the military needed vast amounts of supplies, from food and clothing to bandages and tanks. The government employed the resources of the private sector to produce all of these items; large firms were the preferred choice of the government because they could make more goods in less time. Although small businesses had important contributions to make, they needed help finding ways to be useful. As a result, Congress stepped in and created the Smaller War Plants Corporation (SWPC). In addition to serving as an advocate for small business, the SWPC provided loans to help

Small Business Investment Companies

In the mid-1950s Congress recognized that individual entrepreneurs often lacked the necessary resources to start or expand their own businesses, even if their ideas were sound. In response, Congress created the Small Business Investment Company (SBIC) program. Through this program, the Small Business Administration (SBA) licenses private investment firms to provide venture capital to small and independent businesses. The private investment firms must supply a portion of the money to be invested, and the federal government provides the rest through low-interest loans to the SBICs, who then invest the money in small businesses.

The SBICs have two goals. First, they want to make a profit. They try to invest their money in small businesses that are likely to be successful. Second, they try to help small business owners who have good ideas gain access to the resources that they need. Until 1996 SBICs were of two kinds: regular SBICs and specialized small business investment companies (SSBICs). SSBICs were designed to provide capital to small business owners who faced severe social or economic disadvantages. Congress folded existing SSBICs into the main SBIC program in 1996 and eliminated any further SBIC programs that took race or ethnicity into account.

Overall the program generates a remarkable $4.4 billion of investment each year. Some investments pay off handsomely. For example, Callaway Golf Company, maker of the popular Big Bertha golf clubs, began in 1982 with a personal $400,000 investment by Ely Callaway (his life savings) and a $510,000 investment by an SBIC; since then sales have exceeded $2 billion. Other success stories include Intel (computer chips) and Staples (office products).

small firms invest in materials needed for war production. When World War II ended, so did the SWPC, reemerging in a slightly different form during the Korean War. The new Small Defense Plants Administration (SDPA) certified small businesses to the RFC when they demonstrated that they could properly carry out the terms of a government procurement contract. Energetic support for small businesses in the field of procurement was an essential function of these organizations and has been a central function of the SBA as well.

Since its creation, the SBA has expanded the number and kinds of activities in which it engages to help small business owners. Through its Small Business Development Centers, Business Information Centers, and its Service Corps of Retired Executives, the SBA offers counseling and training as well as technological support to both new and existing small businesses. The Office of Advocacy, an independent branch within the SBA, serves as a liaison and supporter of small business in the policy-making process. The Office of Advocacy pays close attention to federal regulations and suggests ways to reduce the paperwork burden on small business owners. The SBA also licenses more than 350 small business investment companies (SBIC) across the country, which provide venture capital for start-up companies (see box). SBICs are considered to have been partly responsible for the Internet boom of the 1990s. The SBA has made a special

---

Some Small Business Administration Achievements 1999

- Provided capital and credit to 16,144 entrepreneurs to start businesses
- Provided about 11 percent of all outstanding credit to small businesses
- Contracted 41,619 general business loans for $10.2 billion
- Managed a guaranteed-loan portfolio of more than $40.5 billion in loans to 486,000 small businesses
- Helped create 2.3 million of the 15 million new jobs in small business between 1992 and 1998
- Made 3,100 equity investments worth $4.2 billion through venture capital program
- Provided 53 percent of all venture capital financing and 24 percent of total dollar amount of venture capital financing
- Helped small firms receive 22.4 percent of the $200 billion in federal contracts
- Provided 36,000 disaster loans for $1 billion that saved more than 35,000 jobs
- Saved $5.3 billion in costs to small businesses by working with regulatory agencies

Source: Small Business Administration.

---

effort to increase the number of women- and minority-owned small businesses, with programs like the Women's Business Centers and the One Stop Capital Shops.

Overall, nearly 20 million small businesses have received assistance from the SBA since 1953. In 2000 the SBA helped small businesses secure more than $12.3 billion in loans, provided over $1 billion in disaster relief, and assisted small businesses in securing over $40 billion in federal procurement contracts. The SBA remains one of the most important sources of funding for small entrepreneurs.

Small Business Administration Services

- Financial backing
  - Loans
  - Loan guarantees
  - Venture capital
- Advocacy
- Management and technical assistance
- Disaster relief
- Assistance for minority- and women-owned business
- Aid in acquiring federal contracts

Further Reading

Bean, Jonathan. *Beyond the Broker State: Federal Policies toward Small Business, 1936–1961.* Chapel Hill: University of North Carolina Press, 1996.
———. *Big Government and Affirmative Action: The Scandalous History of the Small Business Administration.* Lexington: University of Kentucky Press, 2001.
Parris, Addison W. *The Small Business Administration.* New York: Praeger, 1968.
Zeigler, L. Harmon. *The Politics of Small Business.* Washington, D.C.: Public Affairs Press, 1961.

—McGee Young

Smith, Adam

1723–1790
Economist

Adam Smith is the acknowledged founder of modern economic science (originally known as political economy) and the original theoretician of capitalism. His towering reputation rests on his economic treatise *The Wealth of Nations* (1776).

Smith was born in Kircaldy, Scotland. In 1737, at the age of 14, he entered the University of Glasgow. He graduated at 17 and was awarded a fellowship to study at Balliol College, Oxford, where he remained until his return to Scotland in 1746. He began lecturing on rhetoric at the University of Edinburgh in 1748, and in 1751 he was appointed a professor at Glasgow, first of logic and then, a year later, of moral philosophy.

Smith emerged as one of the leading figures in the Scottish Enlightenment. The Enlightenment was a period of European intellectual development that emphasized reason and experience as the foundations of true knowledge and was confident in incremental human progress through learning. Enlightenment thought was subversive of religion and of traditional social and political institutions, and it generated the liberal ideas of liberty and equality that were to inspire the American and French Revolutions. In Scotland the Enlightenment was pioneered by the philosophers Francis Hutcheson, who taught Smith at Glasgow, and by David Hume, who became one of Smith's most intimate friends.

In 1759 Smith published *The Theory of Moral Sentiments,* in which he set out the ethical theory on which his later economic writings would be based. In the eighteenth century, moral philosophy was divided into two principal schools of thought: the rationalist school, exemplified by the German philosopher Immanuel Kant, believed that moral principles could be discovered through rational thought processes; the rival school of legal positivism, represented by Jeremy Bentham and the English utilitarians, countered that the only standard of right and wrong was the law created by the state itself. In *The Theory of Moral Sentiments*, Smith broke with both interpretations to argue that humans are born with an innate moral sense. He emphasized that people are primarily motivated by self-interest, which must always be recognized by any practical philosophy, yet people are also endowed with a conscience and a capacity for sympathy.

The book was an instant success, quickly establishing Smith's international reputation as a philosopher and bringing him to the attention of the politician Charles Townshend, who hired Smith to tutor his stepson, the young duke of Buccleuch. In 1764 Smith and his charge

An eighteenth-century portrait of Adam Smith.

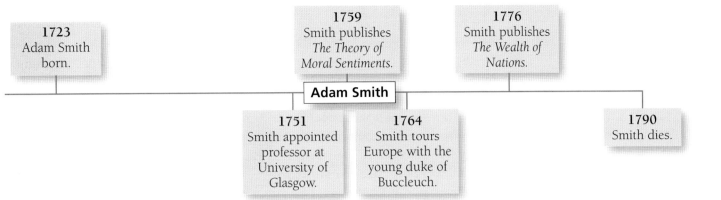

1723
Adam Smith born.

1759
Smith publishes *The Theory of Moral Sentiments.*

1776
Smith publishes *The Wealth of Nations.*

Adam Smith

1751
Smith appointed professor at University of Glasgow.

1764
Smith tours Europe with the young duke of Buccleuch.

1790
Smith dies.

left on an educational tour of Europe, beginning in France. This enabled Smith to exchange ideas with many French intellectuals, including the leading physiocrat François Quesnay. Physiocracy was a school of economic thought that held that agriculture constituted the only real source of wealth creation. Consequently, the physiocrats opposed government encouragement of industrial development and argued for a policy of laissez-faire, or government nonintervention, in economic affairs. Exposure to Quesnay's ideas had a profound effect on the development of Smith's own economic theories. Against the physiocratic position, Smith argued that it was labor, rather than nature, that was the source of value—an idea he had inherited from the seventeenth-century English philosopher John Locke. At the same time, however, Smith was much impressed with the physiocrats' emphasis on free trade, which he was to make central to his own economic thinking.

In 1766 Smith's European tour was cut short by the death of the duke's younger brother. Smith returned to Scotland and began years of strenuous work on *The Wealth of Nations.* The book was written in fundamental opposition to mercantilism, the dominant economic philosophy of the time. In the mercantilist analysis, a country grew in wealth to the extent that it exported more than it imported, and the government must ensure that this positive balance of trade was achieved and maintained. To do so,

governments created monopolies through royal charters and embarked on imperial adventures to secure new markets. The underlying assumption of the mercantilist school was that an increase in the wealth of one state must come at the expense of another state or states.

In *The Wealth of Nations,* Smith developed a radically different theory of wealth creation. His concern was how economic organization could best serve the generality of human needs, rather than the specific needs of vested interests within the state or the state itself. His solution was economic growth—an increase in per capita national income, which would benefit both rich and poor alike. Smith argued that economic growth was best achieved through two principal mechanisms: free market competition and the division of labor.

Smith's theories of political economy flowed from his earlier ethical theories. He held that both the self-interested and cooperative elements of human nature were illustrated and reconciled by our universal propensity to trade. For Smith, the free market was "an invisible hand" that guided an individual's private ambitions toward the unintended promotion of the public good. He wrote that "it is not from the benevolence of the butcher, the brewer, or the baker that we expect our dinner, but from their regard to their self-interest. We address ourselves, not to their humanity, but to their self-love, and never talk to them of our necessities, but of their advantages." People did not produce meat, beer, or bread because they wanted others to have those things; rather, they did it for the rewards that this work brought them personally. In an environment of free competition, producers had incentives to produce the goods people wanted to buy, at a price they were prepared to pay. The result was the empowerment of the consumer. This was in marked contrast to the mercantilist system, under which the state favored selected producers.

In a free market, producers sought to achieve a competitive advantage by raising productivity, defined as output per worker per specified unit of time. Using the example of a pin factory, Smith demonstrated that the principal determinant of productivity was the division of labor into specialized tasks—a regime of work organization that Smith took to be, like trade, a feature common to all human societies. By recognizing that individuals possess different skills, the division of labor allowed workers to concentrate on their respective strengths and to refine their skills to the maximum. As the scope of the free market grew from the local to the national, and then to the international, competitive pressures increased and thereby intensified the degree of specialization in the work process. The result, Smith said, would be an upward spiral of efficiency and innovation that drove the process of wealth creation.

The revolutionary aspect of Smith's economic philosophy was his contention that the wealth of nations depended not on the actions of governments pursuing a grand design, but on the coming together of supply and demand in an endless series of individual transactions entered into without reference to the economic welfare of society as a whole. As a staunch advocate of laissez-faire, Smith held that government intervention in pursuit of certain goals (for example, protecting jobs in a specific industry, or raising the income of workers in a particular occupation) would distort the market, create inefficiencies, and retard economic growth. Only the free market could effectively coordinate the impersonal interdependence of autonomous individuals in a complex society.

Smith's opposition to government intervention in the economy was far from absolute. He argued that government had an important role to play in three areas: the provision of national defense, the administration of justice, and the provision of what economists now call public goods—goods that a private supplier has no market incentive to produce. Consequently, reading Smith as an unqualified critic of government intervention is a mistake. Similarly, interpreting him as merely a champion of the business classes is wrong. Smith flatly denied that the interests of traders and those of the public at large

---

Key Ideas of Adam Smith

- Humans are born with an innate moral sense.
- The human capacity for sympathy, rather than natural law perceived by reason, underlies humankind's ideas of good and evil.
- Self-interest plays a key role in human behavior.
- The human capacity for sympathy protects society against unrestrained self-interest.
- Self-interest, tempered by enlightenment, will benefit society.
- Economic growth is best achieved by free market competition and division of labor.
- National wealth depends not on government programs or the physical possession of large quantities of precious metals but on innumerable individual transactions made without reference to the well-being of society.
- Commercial and industrial activities, not just agriculture, are important in creating national wealth.

Source: Peter Hann Reill, and Ellen Judy Wilson, *Encyclopedia of the Enlightenment,* New York, Facts On File, 1996.

The Theory of Moral Sentiments
(Excerpt)

This disposition to admire, and almost to worship, the rich and the powerful, and to despise, or, at least, to neglect persons of poor and mean condition, though necessary both to establish and to maintain the distinction of ranks and the order of society, is, at the same time, the great and most universal cause of the corruption of our moral sentiments. That wealth and greatness are often regarded with the respect and admiration which are due only to wisdom and virtue; and that the contempt, of which vice and folly are the only proper objects, is often most unjustly bestowed upon poverty and weakness, has been the complaint of moralists in all ages.

We desire both to be respectable and to be respected. We dread both to be contemptible and to be contemned. But, upon coming into the world, we soon find that wisdom and virtue are by no means the sole objects of respect; nor vice and folly, of contempt. We frequently see the respectful attentions of the world more strongly directed towards the rich and the great, than towards the wise and the virtuous. We see frequently the vices and follies of the powerful much less despised than the poverty and weakness of the innocent. To deserve, to acquire, and to enjoy the respect and admiration of mankind, are the great objects of ambition and emulation. Two different roads are presented to us, equally leading to the attainment of this so much desired object; the one, by the study of wisdom and the practice of virtue; the other, by the acquisition of wealth and greatness. Two different characters are presented to our emulation; the one, of proud ambition and ostentatious avidity; the other, of humble modesty and equitable justice. Two different models, two different pictures, are held out to us, according to which we may fashion our own character and behaviour; the one more gaudy and glittering in its colouring; the other more correct and more exquisitely beautiful in its outline. . . .

It is from our disposition to admire, and consequently to imitate, the rich and the great, that they are enabled to set, or to lead what is called the fashion. Their dress is the fashionable dress; the language of their conversation, the fashionable style; their air and deportment, the fashionable behaviour. Even their vices and follies are fashionable; and the greater part of men are proud to imitate and resemble them in the very qualities which dishonour and degrade them. . . .

To attain to this envied situation, the candidates for fortune too frequently abandon the paths of virtue; for unhappily, the road which leads to the one, and that which leads to the other, lie sometimes in very opposite directions. But the ambitious man flatters himself that, in the splendid situation to which he advances, he will have so many means of commanding the respect and admiration of mankind, and will be enabled to act with such superior propriety and grace, that the lustre of his future conduct will entirely cover, or efface, the foulness of the steps by which he arrived at that elevation.

—Adam Smith, *The Theory of Moral Sentiments*, 1759

were identical; he wrote that "People of the same trade seldom meet together, even for merriment and diversion, but the conversation ends in a conspiracy against the public, or in some diversion to raise prices." Such sentiment has been used to justify antitrust legislation and government competition policy, though Smith rightly observed that, in his time, the threat to the public interest lay chiefly in government protection of pacts among merchants.

Adam Smith was, above all things, a practical philosopher. His concern was to develop and clarify a system of political economy that was grounded in the realities of human nature and that could, therefore, function as a guide to public policy. His detractors have focused their criticisms on his conception of human nature, on the inequalities produced by market economies, and on the social consequences of market ethics and culture. However, in terms of the translation of his ideas into practice, Smith is arguably the most accomplished theoretician of the past two centuries.

Further Reading

Fry, Michael, ed. *Adam Smith's Legacy: His Place in the Development of Modern Economics.* London: Routledge, 1992.

Haakonssen, Knud, ed. *Adam Smith.* Aldershot, U.K.: Ashgate, 1998.

Heilbroner, Robert. *The Essential Adam Smith.* New York: W. W. Norton, 1985.

Ross, Ian S., ed. *On The Wealth of Nations: Contemporary Responses to Adam Smith.* Bristol, U.K.: Thoemmes Press, 1998.

Smith, Adam. *The Wealth of Nations.* 1776. Reprint, New York: Everyman's Library, 1991.

—*Peter C. Grosvenor*

See also:
Capitalism; Communism;
Private Property;
Privatization.

Socialism

Socialism is a political ideology that maintains that economic equality is necessary for genuine human freedom. Socialists, accordingly, work to replace the capitalist system of competition and private property with a system based on cooperation and common ownership.

Despite these unifying themes of egalitarianism and anticapitalism, historically socialists have been divided over two main issues. First, reform versus revolution: Could the capitalist system be reformed through the democratic process or must it be overthrown by revolution? Second, collectivist versus libertarian socialism: Should a socialist economy be run by the government or by the workers themselves?

The Origins of Socialism

Socialists sometimes trace their origins to slave uprisings in the classical world, to peasant rebellions against the feudal system, or to the radicalism of the English Civil War in the 1640s. Socialists may draw inspiration from these episodes, yet no identifiable lineage connects these incidents to modern socialist thought, which is a product of the Industrial Revolution.

The term *socialism* was first used in the 1830s to describe the ideas of the utopian socialists Robert Owen, Charles Fourier, and Henri de Saint-Simon. Owen was a Welsh industrialist and social reformer who made three major contributions to the development of socialism: his experiments in collective living and working at New Lanark in Scotland and later New Harmony in Indiana; his theoretical views on the importance of the social environment in the formation of the human character; and his leadership of the first national trade union confederation in Britain. Fourier, a French social theorist, also advocated experimental communities. The creation of small-scale

Plans for New Harmony, Indiana, a utopian socialist community founded by Robert Owen in 1825.

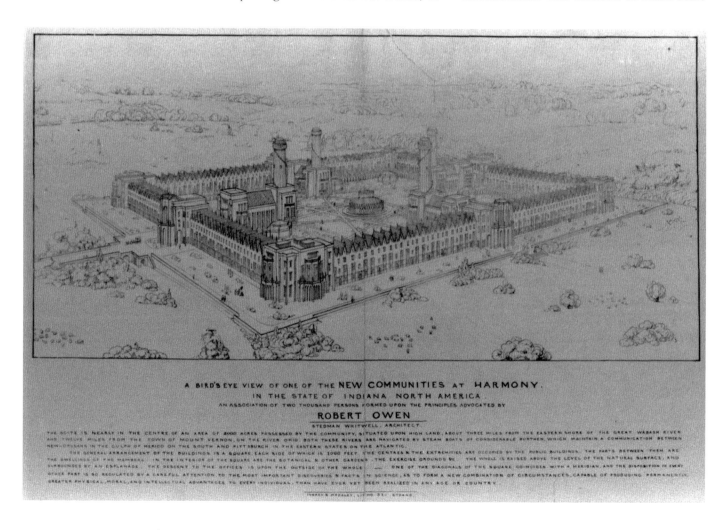

A BIRD'S EYE VIEW OF ONE OF THE NEW COMMUNITIES AT HARMONY.
IN THE STATE OF INDIANA NORTH AMERICA
AN ASSOCIATION OF TWO THOUSAND PERSONS FORMED UPON THE PRINCIPLES ADVOCATED BY
ROBERT OWEN
STEDMAN WHITWELL, ARCHITECT.

Apples being transported from a kibbutz in Israel in the 1980s.

cooperatives has continued to be a part of the libertarian socialist tradition and can still be seen, for example, in the Israeli kibbutz movement. Saint-Simon, another French thinker, took part in both the American and French Revolutions. His ideas on the achievement of social justice through industrialization directed by experts marks the start of collectivist socialism's interest in economic planning.

Marxism

The nineteenth-century German intellectual Karl Marx, along with his collaborator Friedrich Engels, rejected utopian socialism and worked to develop a theory of scientific socialism that would identify the laws of historical development, analyze the nature of capitalist society, and provide a strategy for the achievement of a communist society. They first set out their ideas in *The Communist Manifesto* (1848). Marx advanced three main arguments. First, all societies are divided along class lines. Second, every society has a class of exploiters and exploited. Third, history is driven forward toward communism by class conflict.

Marx contended that in a capitalist society the ruling class uses its economic power to shape society's ideas and culture to disguise the exploitation of the working class. Marx predicted that the capitalist system would impoverish the workers, who would then become receptive to the ideas of communist agitators. In most cases, the capitalists would have to be overthrown in violent revolution. Society would then enter its socialist phase, in which industry would be taken over by the state. In the later communist phase, the state would "wither away" and society would be organized on the principle of "from each according to his capacity, to each according to his needs."

Russia experienced the world's first communist revolution in 1917. Vladimir Lenin, the revolution's leader, was succeeded in 1928 by Joseph Stalin. Stalin initiated a drastic program of forced economic development directed by a totalitarian state. Stalin's exiled rival, Leon Trotsky, developed a Marxist critique of Soviet bureaucracy and organized revolutionary parties to work against state rule and for communist societies based on workers' control. Trotsky was murdered by Stalin's agents in 1940.

The Stalinist model was imposed on Eastern Europe by the Red Army at the close of World War II. Only Yugoslavia successfully pursued a communist path independent of the Soviet Union. In Hungary in 1956 and Czechoslovakia in 1968, attempts by communist governments to assert greater independence from Moscow were militarily thwarted by Soviet invasions.

In 1949 Mao Zedong led the communists to power in China. Mao developed a version of Marxism adapted to the conditions of developing countries, making the peasantry the agents of revolution. Both China and the Soviet Union backed communist parties and guerrilla movements in Asia, Latin America, and Africa. The expanding communist world was substantially weakened, however, by the Sino–Soviet split of the late 1960s, brought about by ideological differences and traditional rivalries between the two great powers.

Communism eventually collapsed in the early 1990s, brought down by its inability to sustain military expenditures, by the immense inefficiencies of its planned economies, and by tensions within the Soviet bloc, especially in Eastern Europe. Most former communist states have since converted to democracy and the market economy, with varying degrees of success. Others have been plagued by ethnic conflict, especially the new republics of the former Yugoslavia. The People's Republic of China has maintained its communist system of government while making the transition to a market economy. Residual communist countries, for example, Cuba and Vietnam, are also liberalizing their economies. Only North Korea remains relatively unchanged.

The Social Democratic Tradition

West European social democracy, or democratic socialism, is a strand of socialist thought that has developed independently of Marxism. Social democrats want to use the democratic process to reform capitalism in the direction of greater equality. They trace their origins to the German socialist Eduard Bernstein and his book *Evolutionary Socialism* (1899). Reformists argue that capitalism has changed since Marx began writing about it in the 1840s. Working men (and later women) have acquired the right to vote. Labor and socialist political parties have emerged. Trade unions have improved workers' pay and conditions. A growing number of worker-capitalists have even bought shares in businesses. Thus, proletarian revolution has become unnecessary, even counterproductive. From the early twentieth century onward, European leftists criticized capitalism increasingly in ethical, rather than economic, terms.

In the years following World War II, most West European countries created comprehensive welfare states (governments that devote a large measure of their expenditures to providing benefits to individuals) and mixed economies (economies that are partly market-driven and partly government-controlled, in which the state takes over key industries). In *The Future of Socialism* (1956), British Labour politician Anthony Crosland argued that socialists had achieved their principal goals; consequently, no further state ownership was

A socialist rally in Madrid, Spain, in 1995.

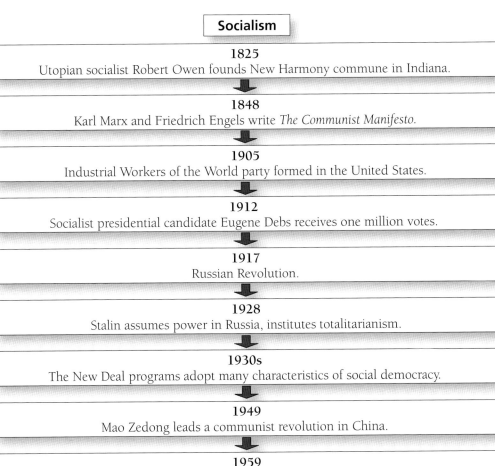

Socialism

1825
Utopian socialist Robert Owen founds New Harmony commune in Indiana.

1848
Karl Marx and Friedrich Engels write *The Communist Manifesto.*

1905
Industrial Workers of the World party formed in the United States.

1912
Socialist presidential candidate Eugene Debs receives one million votes.

1917
Russian Revolution.

1928
Stalin assumes power in Russia, institutes totalitarianism.

1930s
The New Deal programs adopt many characteristics of social democracy.

1949
Mao Zedong leads a communist revolution in China.

1959
German Social Democratic Party renounces Marxism.

1991
Union of Soviet Socialist Republics is dissolved.

1997
Tony Blair becomes prime minister of the United Kingdom, advocating a "Third Way."

necessary, and the Left should instead concentrate on creating a more equal society through the redistribution of wealth by means of taxation and social spending. In 1959 the German Social Democratic Party renounced Marxism and proclaimed that it was now a "people's party," not a "workers' party."

In the mid-1970s the model favored by social democrats was put under severe pressure by concurrent rises in unemployment and inflation. Governments throughout the developed world responded with antiinflationary monetary policies, the privatization of state industries, greater free market competition, and welfare reform. In some countries, Britain, the United States, and Canada among them, these policies were championed by conservative politicians and opposed by social democrats. In Australia, New Zealand, and Spain, the reforms arose from social democratic governments.

At the turn of the twenty-first century, social democrats continue efforts to modernize their ideology. The British Labour Party prime minister Tony Blair has joined with centrist politicians from outside the social democratic tradition, including former U.S. president Bill Clinton, to advocate the "Third Way," which seeks to reconcile the market economy with social justice.

American Socialism
In contrast to most other Western democracies, the United States has never accepted

We are entering tonight upon a momentous campaign. The struggle for political supremacy is not between political parties merely, as appears upon the surface, but at bottom it is a life and death struggle between two hostile economic classes, the one the capitalist, and the other the working class.

The capitalist class is represented by the Republican, Democratic, Populist and Prohibition parties, all of which stand for private ownership of the means of production, and the triumph of any one of which will mean continued wage-slavery to the working class. . . .

The Republican and Democratic parties, or, to be more exact, the Republican-Democratic party, represent the capitalist class in the class struggle. They are the political wings of the capitalist system and such differences as arise between them relate to spoils and not to principles.

With either of those parties in power one thing is always certain and that is that the capitalist class is in the saddle and the working class under the saddle.

Under the administration of both these parties the means of production are private property, production is carried forward for capitalist profit purely, markets are glutted and industry paralyzed, workingmen become tramps and criminals while injunctions, soldiers and riot guns are brought into action to preserve "law and order" in the chaotic carnival of capitalistic anarchy.

Deny it as may the cunning capitalists who are clear-sighted enough to perceive it, or ignore it as may the torpid workers who are too blind and unthinking to see it, the struggle in which we are engaged today is a class struggle, and as the toiling millions come to see and understand it and rally to the political standard of their class, they will drive all capitalist parties of whatever name into the same party, and the class struggle will then be so clearly revealed that the hosts of labor will find their true place in the conflict and strike the united and decisive blow that will destroy slavery and achieve their full and final emancipation.

In this struggle the workingmen and women and children are represented by the Socialist party and it is my privilege to address you in the name of that revolutionary and uncompromising party of the working class. . . .

I shall not stand alone, for the party that has my allegiance and may have my life, the Socialist party, the party of the working class, the party of emancipation, is made up of men and women who know their rights and scorn to compromise with their oppressors; who want no votes that can be bought and no support under any false pretense whatsoever.

The Socialist party stands squarely upon its proletarian principles and relies wholly upon the forces of industrial progress and the education of the working class.

The Socialist party buys no votes and promises no offices. Not a farthing is spent for whiskey or cigars. Every penny in the campaign fund is the voluntary offerings of workers and their sympathizers and every penny is used for education.

What other parties can say the same?

—Eugene Debs, speech to the Socialist Party Convention, 1904

socialism as a mainstream political idea. Historians have suggested several possible explanations. First, as a wealthy society, the United States has avoided some of the material hardships that gave rise to socialist movements elsewhere. Second, America affords greater social mobility than Europe. Consequently, socialism's language of class has less appeal to Americans. Third, during the cold war, communist and socialist ideas were tainted by association with the Soviet Union.

Socialism has not been altogether absent from the American political experience. The late nineteenth century witnessed the growth of radical farmers' movements, principally in the Midwest. A militant trade union movement, the International Workers of the World, known as the Wobblies, was formed in 1905 to achieve socialism through strike action. In the presidential election of 1912, American Socialist Party leader Eugene Debs garnered a million votes; an American Communist Party was founded in 1919.

During the 1930s the Roosevelt administration's New Deal shared many characteristics of social democracy and, in the 1960s, the antipoverty programs of the Kennedy and Johnson administrations owed much to the ideas of the American socialist Michael Harrington. At the beginning of the twenty-first century, Democratic Socialists of America is the principal American affiliate to the social-democratic Socialist International.

Marxist communism has been discredited by its record of political repression and economic failure, and communist parties around the world have gone into decline. By contrast, the social-democratic tradition shows signs of recovery after two decades of serious electoral and ideological challenges. However, whether the advocates of the "Third Way" will revive social democracy or merge it with mainstream liberalism is still to be seen.

Further Reading

Bernstein, Eduard. *Evolutionary Socialism: A Criticism and Affirmation.* Translated by Edith C. Harvey. New York: Schocken Books, 1961.

Crosland, Anthony. *The Future of Socialism.* Westport, Conn.: Greenwood Press, 1977.

Fink, Leon. *Workingmen's Democracy: The Knights of Labor and American Politics.* Urbana: University of Illinois Press, 1983.

Harrington, Michael. *Socialism: Past and Future.* New York: Arcade, 1989.

Kimeldorf, Howard. *Battling for American Labor: Wobblies, Craft Workers, and the Making of the Union Movement.* Berkeley: University of California Press, 1999.

Marx, Karl, and Frederick Engels. *The Communist Manifesto.* 1848. Reprint, New York: Signic Classic, 1998.

—*Peter C. Grosvenor*

Social Security and Medicare

Social security is a complex collection of social programs designed to protect U.S. workers and their families from income losses associated with old age, illness, and death. The Social Security Act, which became law in 1935, has been amended many times and has been adapted to changes in funding and eligibility as well as to shifts in public opinion. Modern social security encompasses Old-Age and Survivors Insurance and Disability Insurance (OASDI) and Medicare, which includes hospital insurance and supplemental medical insurance.

Social security must be distinguished from both welfare and private insurance. Welfare is "means tested" (based on income and need) public assistance to the poor; social security benefits are an earned right unaffected by individuals' assets. Private insurance is a product available only to those who qualify and can afford it; social security is available to virtually all Americans.

Social security operates through a broad trust fund that is derived almost entirely from payroll taxes: contributions are deducted from an earner's paycheck and matched by employers. This money is pooled and used to pay benefits. This money is directed to social security only but is not placed in private accounts for individual workers.

Total benefits received by individuals vary widely and depend on many variables. For example, a low-income worker who is married with several children might become disabled at a young age and receive disability and retirement benefits far exceeding his or her contributions. By contrast, a wealthy single person in good health might delay retirement well beyond 65 and die shortly after retiring, thus receiving only a fraction of what he or she contributed.

History

Most historians and analysts accept that social security was created in response to industrialism. Before 1900 most Americans lived on farms, and the economic security of individuals at all stages of their lives was provided by the extended family and by local charitable institutions. With the Industrial

See also:
Great Depression; New Deal;
Unemployment.

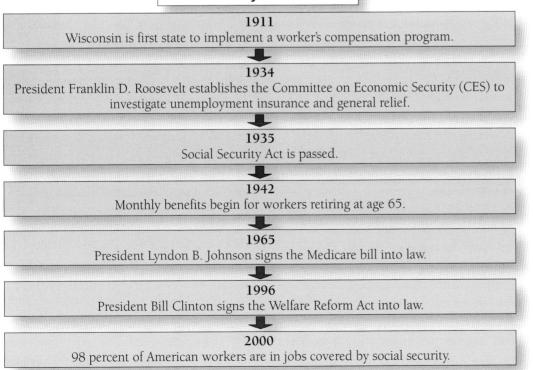

Social Security and Medicare

1911
Wisconsin is first state to implement a worker's compensation program.

1934
President Franklin D. Roosevelt establishes the Committee on Economic Security (CES) to investigate unemployment insurance and general relief.

1935
Social Security Act is passed.

1942
Monthly benefits begin for workers retiring at age 65.

1965
President Lyndon B. Johnson signs the Medicare bill into law.

1996
President Bill Clinton signs the Welfare Reform Act into law.

2000
98 percent of American workers are in jobs covered by social security.

President Franklin D. Roosevelt signs the Social Security Act in 1935. Immediately behind Roosevelt, from left to right, are: Rep. Robert Doughton, Sen. Robert Wagner, Secretary of Labor Frances Perkins, Sen. Pat Harrison, and Rep. David J. Lewis.

Revolution, wage earners became subject to a global industrial economy and often lived far from their families. This shift removed many of society's safety nets. To preserve the benefits of industrialism and to cushion workers against some of its shocks, the United States slowly moved toward a policy of social insurance.

The concept behind social security—that the government is responsible for safeguarding a certain level of economic and social well-being for its people—was fairly new to many Americans in the early part of the twentieth century. However, as early as 1878, several European governments had begun to introduce measures to protect workers from the effects of industrialization. The trend was slower to develop in the United States because of the issue of states' rights, and, some maintain, because of America's cultural bias in favor of self-reliance.

By 1911, however, Wisconsin had implemented a worker's compensation program, and over the next two decades nearly all of the states established some form of worker's compensation. (These programs were and are funded by employer contributions.) Many states had also established unemployment and old-age assistance programs. These programs varied widely, however, and often

had qualification requirements that were hard to meet.

The Great Depression of the 1930s, with its high and chronic unemployment and economic hardships, brought these issues to the fore. President Franklin D. Roosevelt began calling for a relief program early in his first term under the general umbrella of the New Deal. In 1934 Roosevelt established the Committee on Economic Security (CES) to study the matter of both old-age and unemployment insurance and general relief.

What emerged from the CES was the Social Security Act, which allowed substantial federal grants to the states to fund three public assistance programs—Aid to Dependent Children, Old Age Assistance, and Aid to the Blind—and also established two social insurance programs, social security and unemployment insurance. (The latter remained under state control.) The public assistance programs served to provide immediate relief, while social security created a mechanism for providing earned pensions. The act also established the Social Security Board to oversee the program. Roosevelt signed the act into law on August 14, 1935.

Payroll deductions were scheduled to begin in 1937 at a rate of 1 percent from all covered workers and 1 percent from their employers, in accordance with the Federal

Insurance Contributions Act (FICA). At this time coverage was limited to industrial and commercial workers. The first monthly benefits were scheduled to be paid in 1942 to contributing workers who retired at age 65.

Workers retiring between 1937 and 1942 were to be paid a single, lump-sum payment.

In 1939 the act was amended to include dependent children and spouses as beneficiaries. Thus, a worker's benefits would

An advertisement from the Social Security Board from 1935.

continue after death, a change that transformed social security from a retirement program for individuals to a family-based economic security program.

The 1940s were a decade of stagnation for the program. Although the original law called for a gradual tax increase to further build the pension pool, Congress failed to raise the payroll tax and instead raised federal aid to the elderly. In 1946 the Social Security Board was dismantled and the Social Security Administration was established.

The social security system experienced a revival in 1950 during the second term of President Harry S. Truman, when Congress extended coverage to most groups of self-employed workers, including farm workers and small business owners. Benefits were increased by an average of 77 percent to compensate for 15 years of inflation. In 1951, for the first time, the number of social security beneficiaries exceeded the number of people receiving old-age assistance. Social security, not welfare, would define America's approach to financial security in old age.

The Social Security Amendments of 1954, signed by President Dwight D. Eisenhower, initiated a disability insurance program for people age 65 and over, even if they had not worked until retirement age. The age requirement was lowered to

50 two years later. Eventually, permanently disabled workers of any age were able to receive benefits.

The 1961 amendments, signed by President John F. Kennedy, lowered the age at which men were first eligible to receive retirement benefits to 62. (Women had been given this same option in 1956.) Those electing this option accepted a permanent 20 percent reduction in benefits.

President Lyndon B. Johnson signed the Medicare bill into law on July 30, 1965; Medicare brought tremendous changes to America's social insurance system. One of Johnson's Great Society initiatives, this broad health package included three major components: Medicaid, subsidized medicine for most federally assisted welfare recipients; Hospital Insurance, or Medicare Part A, intended for social security retirees; and Supplemental Medical Insurance, known as Medicare Part B, which covered doctors' bills and was also intended for retirees. (Part B was to be funded through general revenues and premiums, not FICA deductions. The program was optional and beneficiaries had to pay extra for it.) The Social Security Administration was responsible for the Medicare program until 1977, after which it was managed by the newly formed Health Care Financing Administration.

Social Security: Beneficiaries, Annual Payments, and Average Monthly Benefits 1990 to 2000

Year	Number of beneficiaries (in thousands)				Annual payments (in million dollars)				Average monthly benefit (in current dollars)		
	Total	Retired workers and dependents	Survivors	Disabled workers and dependents	Total	Retired workers and dependents	Survivors	Disabled workers and dependents	Retired workers	Disabled workers	Widows and widowers
1990	39,832	28,369	7,197	4,266	247,796	172,042	50,951	24,803	$603	$587	$557
1995	43,380	30,139	7,379	5,862	332,581	224,381	67,302	40,898	$720	$682	$680
1997	43,976	30,649	7,171	6,156	361,970	243,590	72,721	45,659	$765	$722	$731
1998	44,247	30,819	7,091	6,338	374,772	252,659	73,940	48,173	$780	$734	$749
1999	44,599	31,035	7,038	6,526	385,525	258,885	75,309	51,331	$804	$755	$775
2000	45,417	31,761	6,981	6,675	407,431	274,645	77,848	54,938	$845	$787	$810

Source: U.S. Social Security Administration, *Social Security Bulletin,* quarterly.

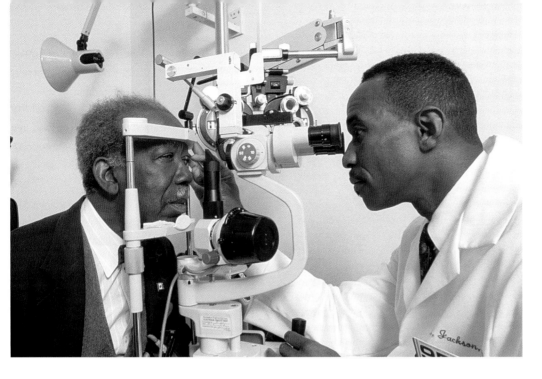

Medicare provides health care for people aged 65 or older, as well as for younger people with disabilities.

Medicare has always used local insurance carriers to make payments to hospitals and doctors. In this way it is like disability insurance because it relies on state intermediaries to administer a federally funded program. Taken together, these programs illustrate an American approach that many feel was necessary to get these laws passed, assuring that states' rights would be protected and that the country would not become a welfare state.

Social security experienced a financial crisis in the 1970s because of a variety of social and economic factors. In 1972 President Richard Nixon signed a law that authorized cost of living allowances that would tie social security benefit amounts to the Consumer Price Index. Unfortunately, benefit amounts rose faster than expected and income was less than anticipated. In response to the crisis, in 1977 President Jimmy Carter convinced Congress to raise both the percentage of the social security tax and the amount of income subject to that tax. Benefits were also scheduled to be reduced slightly. The Amendments of 1980 included provisions that involved greater work incentives for disabled social security beneficiaries.

In response to continuing budget constraints and a lack of public confidence, in 1983 Republicans and Democrats agreed on a series of compromises that left social security largely intact and financially stable for the next several decades: the retirement age would gradually be raised to 67; some social security benefits would be taxed; the reserve would be increased; and coverage would be extended to federal employees. Strategies to control Medicare costs were also implemented.

In 1996, when President Bill Clinton signed the Welfare Reform Act, rules for

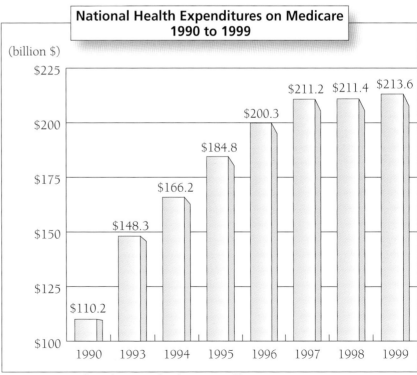

National Health Expenditures on Medicare 1990 to 1999

(billion $)

1990	$110.2
1993	$148.3
1994	$166.2
1995	$184.8
1996	$200.3
1997	$211.2
1998	$211.4
1999	$213.6

Source: U.S. Centers for Medicare & Medicaid Services, *Health Care Financing Review,* summer 2001.

A rally in Washington, D.C., on behalf of Medicare in 1995.

qualifying for SSI and disability were tightened. In 1999 the Ticket to Work and Work Incentives Improvement Act provided disability beneficiaries with vouchers to purchase vocational rehabilitation, employment, and other services in an effort to return them to the workforce. The act also provided incentive payments to service providers when a beneficiary was successfully returned to work.

Enduring Issues

Since social security was established, a number of policy questions have been present in national debate, returning again and again in varying guises. A core issue for social insurance programs is equity versus adequacy. Should social security be a pay-as-you-go system in which one's benefits are largely in line with one's contributions? This would be more equitable. Or should the programs seek to provide a firm income floor under which no citizen should drop? This would be more adequate.

Another debate centers on financing. Do the programs have enough money to honor their promises? If reserves are high, should the surplus be spent by increasing benefits and expanding the program or should the surplus be maintained? If reserves are low, how should money be raised to finance the shortfall—by tax increases, a reduction in benefits, or by other means?

The question of fairness is another pervasive issue surrounding social security. For example, although benefits for low-income earners represent a greater percentage of their preretirement income, high-income earners still receive benefits, even though they may be quite wealthy after retirement. Others see problems in that housewives receive no credit for their work and that some generations bear greater tax burdens than others.

The fundamental structural reality driving the need for some kind of social security reform is that the U.S. population is aging, resulting in a declining ratio of current earners to current beneficiaries. Some analysts have put forward dire forecasts that the system will run out of money and collapse under the burden of too many retirees. A late-twentieth- and early-twenty-first-century debate surrounding social security is the question of privatization, with increased individual control over the funds collected. Some have argued that social security funds should be put into private, individual accounts and even invested in the stock market, although the corporate scandals and severe stock market decline of 2001–2002 appear to have weakened some popular support for that plan.

In 2000 one in six Americans—approximately 45 million people—received a social security benefit and about 98 percent of workers were in jobs covered by social security. In 2000 the fund for OASDI alone saw an income of approximately $565.7 billion, an outgo of $410.3 billion, and a year-end fund balance of $1,051.5 billion. A 2000 report stated that social security could pay full benefits only until 2037.

Further Reading

Eliot, Thomas H. *Recollections of the New Deal.* Boston: Northeastern University Press, 1992.

Kingson, Eric R., and Edward D. Berkowitz. *Social Security and Medicare: A Policy Primer.* Westport, Conn.: Auburn House, 1993.

Schieber, Sylvester J., and John B. Shoven. *The Real Deal: The History and Future of Social Security.* New Haven, Conn.: Yale University Press, 1999.

Social Security Administration. *Fast Facts and Figures about Social Security.* Washington, D.C.: Government Printing Office, 2000.

—*Barbara Gerber*

Sony Corporation

Sony began in the years following World War II as a partnership between electronics engineer Masaru Ibuka and physics graduate Akio Morita. The Tokyo-headquartered multinational is now a powerhouse in the entertainment business, providing record albums and films, electronic gadgets, and online gaming. In fiscal year 2002 Sony reported annual sales of more than $56.9 billion—$18.2 billion in sales in the United States alone.

Ibuka and Morita met during World War II while doing research for the Japanese navy. In 1947 Morita joined Ibuka in Tokyo, bringing capital from his wealthy family, and they formed the Tokyo Tsushin Kogyo K.K. (Tokyo Telecommunications Engineering Corporation; TTEC). The TTEC began by making replacement parts for phonographs, mixing units, and other audio equipment.

In 1952 Ibuka toured AT&T's Bell Laboratories in the United States and saw the newly invented transistor. He realized that replacing the large, clumsy vacuum tube with the transistor would make possible smaller, more portable radios and TVs. Ibuka and Morita immediately saw the potential and licensed the transistor patent. By 1957 they had adapted the transistor for use in the world's first pocket-sized, battery-powered radio.

The huge success of the transistor radio allowed TTEC to expand globally. First the company needed a name that was shorter, snappier—and less Japanese. Morita and Ibuka combined the Latin word *sonus*, meaning sound, with the then-current American slang word *sonny* to make Sony—suggesting a company made up of young people with abundant energy.

In February 1960 Sony established Sony Corporation of America. Morita and his family moved to New York to run this new American division. The following year Sony became the first Japanese company to offer stock in the United States, paving the way for other Japanese companies to begin raising foreign capital.

The Forward March of the Television

Sony was unique in that it could anticipate tastes and create the right products, even before consumers realized what they wanted. For example, in 1968 Sony introduced the Trinitron KV-1310 color television. The Trinitron used transistors instead of vacuum tubes to produce a clear, bright color picture. It immediately became the industry standard for color television sets.

See also:
Arts and Entertainment Industry; Morita, Akio; Multinational Corporation.

In June 1960 Akio Morita, right, signs documents concerning the company's scheduled public offering in the United States of 200,000 American shares; Sony was the first Japanese company to sell stock in the United States. Ernest B. Schwarzenbach, left, partner of the underwriting firm of Smith, Barney, and Teruo Kurata, standing, managing director of Nomura Securities, watch the signing.

Morita's keen understanding of the American consumer is also evident in his design of the Walkman (first marketed in 1979). Morita realized that consumers wanted a more portable stereo after watching his children and their friends play music from morning until night and noticing how people were willing to lug large stereos around to the beach and the park. By the 1990s the Walkman had become as much a part of everyday teenage life as the transistor radio had been for the previous generation.

Of course, Morita's vision could not guarantee success every time. The first videotape recorder was developed by the Ampex Corporation in 1956. The reel-to-reel machine was the size of a small car and used tape that was two inches wide. In 1971 Sony designed the U-Matic, a recorder that used ¾-inch tape in a cassette. Four years later Sony created the Betamax—the first videocassette recorder (VCR) that was small enough for home use. (The word *beta* is similar to a Japanese word that refers to a brushstroke in painting or calligraphy that is rich and full, without skips or white spots.)

Shortly after Sony introduced the Betamax, Japan Victor Company (JVC) and its parent company Matsushita Electric introduced their own format called video home system (VHS). The VHS used a different recording format, tape-handling mechanisms, and cassette sizes. Soon the two formats were battling for supremacy. The Betamax eventually lost to the VHS for several reasons. Chief among them was the lack of prerecorded Beta movies and Sony's refusal to license its products to other manufacturers. Crucial alliances with companies like RCA in the United States and Matsushita in Japan were lost and went to the VHS camp. By the end of the 1980s, with sales plummeting, Sony and other Beta manufacturers stopped production of the Betamax VCRs.

The Columbia Tri-Star Reverse

The loss of the VCR wars forced Morita to realize that content was critical to the success of consumer electronics products. Consequently, Sony began acquiring music and movie properties. Sony had already entered the record business in 1968 by establishing CBS/Sony Group jointly with CBS, a U.S. company. In 1988–1989 Sony acquired the world's largest record company, CBS Records.

To Western observers Sony had always seemed like a bottom-line-oriented conglomerate. However, upper management at Sony still operated via intense personal relationships and loyalties. Sony's decision to buy Columbia Pictures Entertainment in 1989 illustrates how this old-fashioned management structure still existed in one of the world's most globally oriented companies. Morita initially believed

Sony Corporation

1947
Masaru Ibuka and Akio Morita form the Tokyo Telecommunications Engineering Corporation (TTEC).

1957
TTEC creates the world's first pocket-size, battery-powered radio.

1960
Sony Corporation of America established.

1968
Sony forms CBS/Sony Group.

1979
Sony first markets the Walkman.

1988
Sony acquires CBS Records, Columbia Records, and Epic Records.

2002
Sony expands into online gaming and mobile telecommunications.

that Columbia's price was exorbitant and abandoned the idea of the acquisition at a company meeting. At a board dinner later that same evening, Morita voiced regret over the lost opportunity. The next day, the company's directors reconvened and decided that Sony would purchase Columbia after all.

Columbia was dogged by mismanagement and flops for years, and Sony was forced to write off more than $3 billion in losses. A management consolidation, expansion into foreign markets, and a string of hits starting in the mid-1990s eventually propelled Columbia and Sony's entire movie division into the black. Although personal loyalty led to an unwise purchase, Sony's global perspective eventually saved the company. The hit film *Crouching Tiger, Hidden Dragon* (2001) illustrates this perfectly. The film was developed in Taiwan by Sony Pictures Classics, together with Sony Pictures China. The soundtrack was produced by Sony Music and features Sony Music artist Yo-Yo Ma, but the film was produced and filmed locally in China, in hopes of appealing to Chinese, as well as American, moviegoers. *Crouching Tiger* went on to become the highest-grossing non-U.S. film in history.

The Networking Era

In 1993 Morita suffered a stroke and retired as chairman and CEO of Sony. He was replaced by Norio Ohga. When Ohga retired six years later, he selected someone from the new generation—Nobuyuki Idei—to succeed him as president and chief executive officer. Idei was a surprise choice to many in Tokyo who regarded him as a nontechnical heretic in Sony's corporate culture.

Idei began preparing Sony for what he calls "the network-centric era." He believes that the future involves mastering the emerging broadband world to develop interconnected products. The PlayStation is one example of this vision. The game console, first developed in 1993, has become one of Sony's hottest-selling products, accounting for 10 percent of all sales. Sony's goal is to use broadband connectivity to complete home entertainment systems, bringing music and

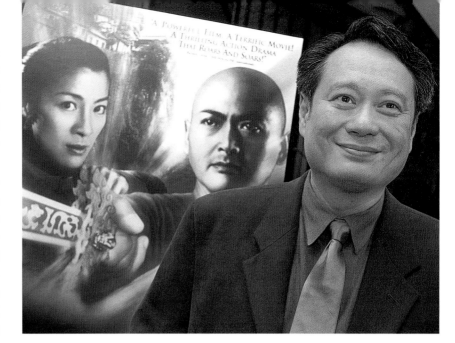

Ang Lee, director of Sony's highly successful feature film Crouching Tiger, Hidden Dragon, *poses at a press event for the film.*

pictures to a Sony-made digital television, a Sony-made wireless device, a PlayStation2 console (with attached hard drive), and a Sony computer.

Sony has also moved into mobile telecommunications with the 2002 launch of 3G, which is a new mode of data-transmission architecture, a wireless and completely portable system that allows users to be online all the time, turning the cell phone into a minicomputer. Sony is also expanding on the Internet, with innovative concepts in online gaming. Sony's online game EverQuest has more than 300,000 paying subscribers, and the company has also launched an online game based on the *Star Wars* films.

Further Reading

Asakura, Reiji. *Revolutionaries at Sony: The Making of the Sony Playstation and the Visionaries Who Conquered the World of Video Games.* New York: McGraw-Hill, 2000.

Cusumano, Michael A., Yiorgos Mylonadis, and Richard S. Rosenbloom. "Strategic Maneuvering and Mass-market Dynamics: The Triumph of VHS over Beta." *Business History Review* (Spring 1992).

Griffin, Nancy, and Kim Masters. *Hit and Run: How Jon Peters and Peter Guber Took Sony for a Ride in Hollywood.* New York: Simon & Schuster, 1997.

Morita, Akio, Edwin M. Reingold, and Mitsuko Shimomura. *Made in Japan.* New York: Dutton, 1986.

Nathan, John. *Sony: The Private Life.* Boston: Houghton Mifflin, 1999.

—Lisa Magloff

Southwest Airlines

Airlines are conventional businesses. Most companies in the industry work in the same basic way, focusing most of their energy on efficiency and profits, with many achieving three related results. First, many employees feel underpaid and unappreciated. Second, most airlines neglect customer service and face common complaints, including those associated with flight delays, lost luggage, prices, and bad food. Third, they frequently lose money. Southwest Airlines operates counter to the traditional ways of its industry, creating its own special recipe for success that has led it to profitability, customer satisfaction, and a unique corporate culture that has made Southwest one of the most popular companies to work for in the United States.

The company began in the classic entrepreneurial manner. In 1967 Hugh Rollins, the operator of a small airline in San Antonio, Texas, saw an opportunity. Travel between the three major cities of Texas—Houston, Dallas, and San Antonio—was inconvenient and expensive. He convinced a local attorney, Hugh Kelleher, to join him in creating an airline to serve this market.

Their initial plan was simple: start an airline that provided direct flights between just these three cities. Beginning with one aircraft, they flew from one destination to the next in a triangular course. Flights were under two hours, which was convenient for customers. Although done from necessity, this approach was Southwest's first departure from industry norms. Most companies in the industry use the hub-and-spoke system, originating most of their flights from a central location. Passengers rarely fly directly to their destination, rather they change planes at the hub.

The hub system has several advantages: the maintenance and catering equipment can be located at the hub, thus reducing expenses; the airline can offer a greater variety of destinations because customers can transfer to any of the spokes leading off the hub, which is usually at a major airport. Flaws include longer travel times and increased delays if the hub is congested.

Southwest faced several problems in its first years of operation. It was founded in 1967 but did not fly until 1971 because of legal disputes. When Southwest did finally start to serve customers, competitors attempted to put it out of business by matching its low fares. Overcoming these obstacles forced the company to develop unique business practices that contributed to its great success.

Southwest solved its problems by turning traditional business logic on its head. The company asserted that the employee, not the customer, was always right. Southwest created an environment where the workers were encouraged to enjoy their jobs and feel like they were part of a family; in 1974 the company

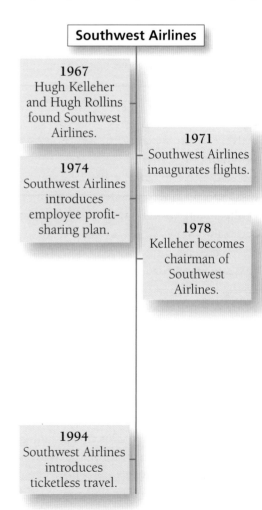

Southwest Airlines

1967
Hugh Kelleher and Hugh Rollins found Southwest Airlines.

1971
Southwest Airlines inaugurates flights.

1974
Southwest Airlines introduces employee profit-sharing plan.

1978
Kelleher becomes chairman of Southwest Airlines.

1994
Southwest Airlines introduces ticketless travel.

Southwest Airlines cofounder and chief executive Herb Kelleher, right, president Colleen Barrett, center, and chief executive officer James Parker pose at company headquarters in Dallas, Texas, on March 19, 2001.

introduced an employee profit-sharing plan, the first U.S. airline to do so. Pilots often used humor while making announcements, flight attendants wore Halloween costumes, and senior management shared meals with "other" workers. This approach helped create a positive atmosphere where all employees actively contributed to making the airline profitable. Eventually, the company reinforced this idea by giving employees stock as a standard benefit. Because they owned part of the company, workers had a stake in its success.

The company extended this democracy to customers through two innovations. In contrast to industry practice, seats are not assigned to each ticket but by order of purchase. Early buyers get low numbers and seat themselves first in a place of their choosing. Southwest also has a simplified pricing structure. Many airlines try to maximize profits by using sophisticated computer software to predict business. Fares change constantly for the same flight, which can lead to some customers feeling that they have overpaid. Southwest offers a simple set of prices and avoids this problem.

Southwest capitalized on its unique atmosphere by including it in its marketing. Early ads featured smiling flight attendants and suggested that Southwest was fun. It also gained national attention by painting one of its planes with the image of Shamu, a killer whale. Shamu was the mascot of a major San Antonio tourist attraction, Sea World, and was part of a campaign to encourage vacation travel to that city.

In another example, Kelleher, who had become chairman of the company in 1978, employed a novel method to solve a legal problem. Southwest had been sued by another airline, which was using a similar slogan. Rather than spending years in litigation, the chairmen of the companies agreed to solve their dispute through arm wrestling. Even though he lost to a much younger man, Southwest gained valuable publicity and maintained its reputation as a maverick in the industry.

Southwest's methods have stood the test of time. Focusing on happy employees increased productivity and helped Southwest win multiple customer service awards. The company became profitable

A Southwest Airlines jet on final approach at Lindbergh Field in San Diego, California.

enough to expand steadily into new markets. As it grew, the airline continued to innovate along its basic business model of low prices and direct flights. One of the keys to its success is operating at smaller airports around major cities. An example is its use of Midway Airport in Chicago rather than the much busier O'Hare. Smaller airports are less crowded and tend to be closer to customers.

A more recent innovation is the company's embrace of new technology. Southwest introduced ticketless travel in 1994, and it was a leader in use of the Internet to sell tickets. These innovations added convenience for customers and cut the commissions the company must pay to travel agents.

Southwest Airlines has demonstrated that business success can be had by challenging traditional wisdom. The company has grown to become the fifth largest airline in the United States, serving 57 cities, carrying 57 million passengers on more than 2,600 flights per year. While other airlines struggle with profits and unhappy customers, Southwest continues to succeed and expand.

Further Reading

Doganis, Rigas. *The Airline Business in the Twenty-first Century*. New York: Routledge, 2001.

Freiberg, Kevin, and Jackie Freiberg. *Nuts! Southwest Airlines' Crazy Recipe for Business and Personal Success*. Austin, Tex.: Bard Press International, 1996.

—David Long

Sports Industry

The Boston Red Sox were sold for $660 million in 2002. Counting tournament winnings and endorsements, golfer Tiger Woods earned $53 million in 2001. National Football League owners will pocket $18.7 billion over eight seasons from selling television rights. These numbers—and many more could be added—testify to the prosperity of the sports industry. Americans are avid sports fans, but their passions only partly explain why the business has boomed since 1950. Rising incomes, more leisure, increased urbanization, and the growing power of television have fueled the growth of sports and other recreational activities.

Government statistics cannot provide a clear measure of the industry's size. Sports spending is scattered among a half-dozen or so industries, intermingled with clothing stores and amusement parks. The Census Bureau estimates that spectator sports, including professional leagues and events, earned $19 billion in revenue in 2000. The category, however, fails to capture large segments of the business, including radio and television receipts, equipment sales, and gambling. Street & Smith's *SportsBusiness Journal*, an industry publication, offers a broader estimate of the industry—$194.6 billion in revenue in 2001. The major components were advertising at $27.4 billion, spectator spending at $26.2 billion, sporting goods at $25.6 billion, team and event operating expenses at $23 billion, gambling at $18.9 billion, and sales of licensed merchandise at $10.5 billion.

Although sports is a big business, many of the individual enterprises are not large. In 2001 revenues of the New York Yankees, the richest baseball team, totaled $242.2 million, hardly Fortune 500 numbers. At the other end of the industry, struggling just to stay in business, are small-time hockey teams and dirt-track race-car drivers.

Business Models

Baseball, football, basketball, hockey, and other team sports usually organize themselves into leagues, which grant franchises and organize season-long competitions. Teams operate as independent businesses by signing players, selling tickets, and advertising. Since 1960 league offices have expanded

See also:
Arts and Entertainment Industry; Major League Baseball Players Association; Recreation Industry.

The Staples Center in downtown Los Angeles has hosted two NBA championships. A sports-themed advertisement for Apple Computer is featured on the side of the Hotel Figueroa.

their business roles, with national television contracts, sponsorship, and licensing.

A different business model reigns in individual sports—golf, tennis, boxing, and automobile racing. Sanctioning bodies, for example, the National Association for Stock Car Auto Racing (NASCAR) and the Professional Golfers Association (PGA), run the competitions, making money through fees and sponsorships. Promoters stage events, taking responsibility for venues, marketing, ticket sales, and prize money. Competitors are essentially independent contractors, whose earnings are based on performance as well as the ability to attract sponsors.

The industry offers variations on the basic models. Collegiate and amateur sports sell tickets, television rights, and licensed merchandise, but they do not pay market wages to athletes. Horseracing derives most of its revenue from gambling. ESPN, the cable network, owns the X Games, a competition for skateboarding, bicycle stunts, and other daredevil sports.

The era of free agency sent players' salaries soaring. The industry responded with a new organizational structure—the single-entity league. Owners buy shares in a league, not individual franchises. The central office sets pay scales and signs players, so teams no longer vie for talent. In 2000 Major League Soccer, the largest single-entity sport, won a lawsuit in which players charged that central control violated antitrust laws.

Only Major League Baseball enjoys antitrust exemption, but arrangements to restrict economic competition are commonplace in sports. Leagues limit the number of franchises, grant exclusive territorial rights, and cap roster size. Even in the era of free agency, leagues still limit competition in the labor market by conducting drafts for incoming players and granting teams exclusive negotiating rights during the early years of athletes' careers.

Most professional sports are dominated by one league or organization. Nevertheless, sports monopolies are not absolute. NASCAR runs stock car racing, but two groups offer the open-wheeled racing made popular by the Indianapolis 500. In 1971 antitrust suits ended the National Basketball Association's draft rules that kept out younger players; similar lawsuits ended the National Collegiate Athletic Association's control of college football telecasts in 1984. Rivals emerge from time to time—for example, the American Football League from 1960 to 1969. Direct competition kicks off bidding wars for players, eventually leading upstart leagues to fold or merge into existing organizations.

New Revenue Streams

As sports boomed, both league and individual competitions saw strong growth in traditional revenue streams—ticket sales, stadium signage, concessions, parking, souvenirs, and radio and television broadcasting. The National Football League's (NFL) network television receipts, for example, jumped from an average of $470 million a year in the 1987–1989 contracts to $2.2 billion a year in the deal that runs from 1998 to 2005.

The rising costs of buying franchises and signing top players have pushed sports enterprises to seek new revenue streams. Since the early 1990s, they have turned increasingly to their stadiums and arenas. Teams sold naming rights for ever-higher fees; for example, the Houston Texans will receive $300 million over 30 years from Reliant Energy Company,

Careers in the Sports Industry

Great athletic ability is not the only route to earning a living in sports and related businesses. Teams, event organizers, sports facilities, college athletic departments, and city sports commissions offer a variety of employment opportunities—from administration to ticket sales and marketing, from public relations to customer service and merchandising.

Since about 1990, sports marketing has emerged as a specialty of its own. Anheuser Busch Company and others hire their own staffs and handle the job in-house. Other companies rely on outside sports-marketing companies.

Furthermore, although the spotlight shines on the big leagues, the minor leagues and niche sports often provide entry-level jobs. They are often willing to give young people responsibility for ticketing, marketing, or other key functions.

By tradition, sports were largely family-run businesses, where finding employment involved connections and learning on the job. With the industry growing more complex, employers are looking for specialized skills and training. The need for expertise has led some colleges and universities to create sports-related curricula. Seton Hall University, the University of Massachusetts, Ohio University, and dozens of other schools offer degree programs ranging from sports administration to sports law.

Soccer teams D.C. United and Los Angeles Galaxy squared off in the 1999 Major League Soccer Championship. In 2000 the league won a lawsuit brought by players that charged that the league was in violation of antitrust laws.

which named the team's stadium Reliant Stadium. A novelty in the 1970s, naming rights had spread to nearly all facilities by the end of the 1990s. New stadiums included club seats, providing restaurants, bars, and other amenities at higher prices. The Chicago Bulls and Chicago Blackhawks charged as much as $300,000 in 2001 for one of the 212 luxury suites in the United Center. The same year, the Washington Redskins' club seats sold for up to $2,695 for an eight-game season. The suites and club seats increased revenues, but they made sports more dependent on corporate customers.

As teams decided they needed new facilities to stay competitive, professional sports embarked on its greatest building boom. Including major renovations and facilities under construction, the professional sports franchises will have built 69 new stadiums and arenas between 1990 and 2005, a $20 billion investment. At least 13 other major league teams are campaigning for new facilities. At the same time, top colleges are emulating their big-league relations, adding luxury suites and club seats.

Sports facilities have grown more elaborate and expensive as they have become cash cows for franchises. Features like retractable roofs, cigar bars, and health clubs are becoming more common. From 1999 to 2002, Seattle and its teams spent nearly $1 billion for new sports facilities—$517 million in baseball and $430 million in football.

In sports' early years, owners paid for their own stadiums and arenas. Now, most sports facilities receive taxpayer subsidies. Owners campaign for public funds by persuading local and state governments that hosting big league teams adds to a city's prestige and stimulates economic development.

Critics decry the subsidies for sports owners, some of them the richest people in the country. Robert Baade, a professor at

Lake Forest College in Illinois, and other researchers have produced study after study showing that host cities do not receive an economic windfall from sports facilities. After failing five times to win public support, the San Francisco Giants financed their own $255 million ballpark, opened in 1999. For the most part, though, teams have succeeded in securing public support for new facilities.

Sports Stars Growing Richer

Athletes shared in sports' prosperity as pay and perks skyrocketed, fueled by television and corporate money. Golfer Tom Watson

Selected Spectator Sports 1985 to 1999						
	Unit	1985	1990	1995	1997	1999
Baseball, major leagues[1]						
Attendance	1,000	47,742	55,512	51,288	64,921	71,061
Regular season	1,000	46,824	54,824	50,469	63,168	70,139
Playoffs[2]	1,000	591	479	533	1,349	706
World Series	1,000	327	209	286	404	216
Players' salaries: average[3]	$1,000	371	598	1,111	1,337	1,607
Basketball[4,5]						
NCAA—Men's college						
Teams	Number	753	767	868	865	932
Attendance	1,000	26,584	28,741	28,548	27,738	29,025
NCAA—Women's college						
Teams	Number	746	782	864	879	956
Attendance	1,000	2,072	2,777	4,962	6,734	8,698
Professional[6]						
Teams	Number	23	27	27	29	29
Attendance, total[7]	1,000	11,534	18,586	19,883	21,677	13,450
Regular season	1,000	10,506	17,369	18,516	20,305	12,135
Average per game	Number	11,141	15,690	16,727	17,077	16,738
Average salaries	$1,000	325	750	1,900	2,200	3,000
Football						
NCAA College[5]						
Teams	Number	509	533	565	581	601
Attendance	1,000	34,952	35,330	35,638	36,858	39,483
National Football League[8]						
Teams	Number	28	28	30	31	32
Attendance, total[9]	1,000	14,058	17,666	19,203	19,050	20,763
Regular season	1,000	13,345	13,960	15,044	14,967	16,207
Postseason games	1,000	711	848	NA	NA	794
Average salary[10]	$1,000	194	352	714	725	1,081
Hockey						
National Hockey League[11]						
Regular season attendance	1,000	11,634	12,580	9,234	17,641	17,995
Playoffs attendance	1,000	1,108	1,356	1,329	1,495	1,472

NA = Not available.

Notes and sources: [1] The National League of Professional Baseball Clubs, National League Green Book, and the American League of Professional Baseball Clubs, American League Red Book, New York. [2] Beginning in 1996, two rounds of playoffs were played. Prior years had one round. [3] Major League Baseball Players Association, New York. [4] Season ending in year shown. [5] National Collegiate Athletic Association, Overland Park, Kan. [6] National Basketball Assn., New York. [7] Includes All-Star game, not shown separately. [8] National Football League, New York. [9] Beginning 1987 includes preseason attendance, not shown separately. [10] National Football League Players Association, Washington, D.C. [11] National Hockey League, Montreal, Quebec.

prevailed in six tournaments in 1980 to finish as professional golf's top money winner with $530,808. Tiger Woods pocketed $5.7 million in taking five titles in 2001. Woods boosted his income ninefold with deals to advertise Nike golf equipment, American Express financial services, Buick cars, and other products. Athletes even did well in emerging sports; for example, in-line skaters can realize $200,000 and more from winnings and endorsements.

For nearly a century, sports leagues had reduced competition for labor through the so-called reserve clause, first imposed in baseball in the 1880s. The practice gave teams exclusive rights to employ players for their entire careers. The arrival of free agency in the 1970s, coupled with rapidly rising revenues, has sent salaries higher.

Between 1990 and 2001, average annual salaries rose from $823,000 to $4.2 million in basketball, from $597,000 to $2.1 million in baseball, from $271,000 to $1.4 million in hockey, and from $430,000 to $1.2 million in football. The top of the market became even more expensive: the Texas Rangers signed shortstop Alex Rodriguez to a 10-year contract worth $252 million.

Rising salaries led to confrontations between owners and players' unions. Strikes and lockouts hit all major team sports, leading to disillusioned fans and canceled games, including the World Series in 1994. Sports owners claimed their businesses were losing money, despite revenue increases and strong gains in franchise values. In testimony before Congress, baseball commissioner Bud Selig said his sport's 30 teams lost a total of $519 million. Economists and labor leaders have not been persuaded. They argue that the sports industry shows few of the usual signs of an industry in distress, for example, bankruptcies and declining asset values. Franchise values soared in the 1990s: the Dallas Cowboys was sold for $150 million in 1989, and the Houston Texans paid a record $700 million to enter the NFL for the 2002 season.

Affordability arose as an issue for average fans. According to *Team Marketing Report,* ticket prices doubled in the four major team sports from 1991 to 2001. NFL tickets jumped from an average of $25.21 to $53.64. Add the cost of food, parking, and souvenirs and a family of four would spend an average of $303 to attend an NFL game.

At a news conference in 2000, shortstop Alex Rodriguez announces he has signed a 10-year, $252 million contract with the Texas Rangers—the largest sum for a single player to that date.

Further Reading

Leeds, Michael, and Peter Von Allmen. *The Economics of Sports.* Boston: Addison-Wesley, 2002.

Noll, Roger G., and Andrew Zimbalist, eds. *Sports, Jobs, and Taxes: The Economic Impact of Sports Teams and Stadiums.* Washington, D.C.: Brookings Institution Press, 1997.

Quirk, James, and Rodney D. Fort. *Pay Dirt: The Business of Professional Team Sports.* Princeton, N.J.: Princeton University Press, 1992.

Rosentraub, Mark S. *Major League Losers: The Real Cost of Sports and Who's Paying for It.* New York: Basic Books, 1997.

Sheehan, Richard G. *Keeping Score: The Economics of Big-Time Sports.* South Bend, Ind.: Diamond Communications, 1996.

Zimbalist, Andrew. *Unpaid Professionals: Commercialism and Conflict in Big-Time College Sports.* Princeton, N.J.: Princeton University Press, 2001.

—*Richard Alm*

Standard of Living

The term *standard of living* is an economic description of the quality of human existence that is subjective and imprecise. It describes the relationships among people's earnings, their desires, their purchases, and their resulting quality of life. Standard of living can encompass a number of topics including income, purchasing power, living conditions, and personal aspirations. To give the best description of how people really live, any description should consider the value systems and circumstances of the time and place. Because of this complexity, standard of living is without a hard-and-fast definition.

The most concrete aspect of standard of living is per capita income, a measure widely accepted by economists and policy analysts as an indicator of an area's economic well-being. Per capita income is determined by dividing the sum of wage and salary disbursements by the number of workers. According to the U.S. Bureau of the Census, per capita income in 2001 was $30,205. Consider the vast difference between that figure and the per capita income of $11,793 in 1968.

Those figures do not reflect the amount of money an average worker had to spend. Analysts frequently subtract the amount people pay in taxes to determine per capita disposable income. Adjustments can also be made for the cost of living, resulting in real per capita disposable income.

Although adjusted figures give some indication of standard of living, employment features beyond salary also contribute to standard of living. Some jobs come with fringe benefits, those small and large financial bonuses provided to the

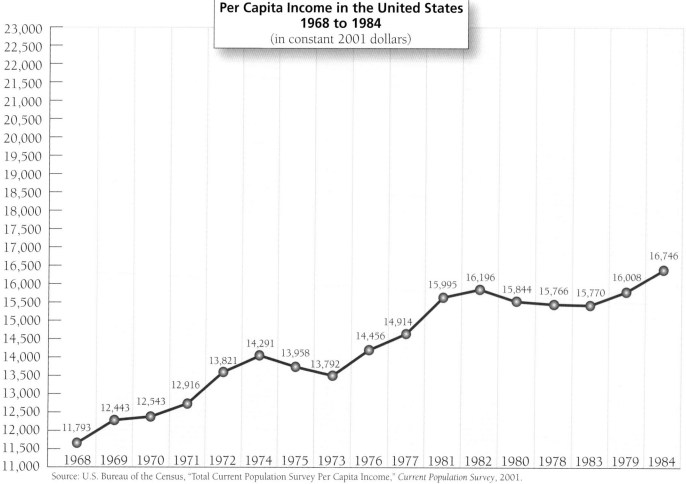

Per Capita Income in the United States 1968 to 1984
(in constant 2001 dollars)

Source: U.S. Bureau of the Census, "Total Current Population Survey Per Capita Income," *Current Population Survey*, 2001.

workers beyond their ordinary salaries. Paid vacations, health insurance, severance pay, stock options, and retirement benefits all offer nonsalary financial boosts to the quality of workers' lives.

Throughout the world, local tastes and habits and even the availability of products have a marked influence on standard of living. In France, for example, wine is considered a staple, and most working adults enjoy quality wine with their dinners, with good wine available at the corner grocery for as little as $2.00 per bottle. In the United States good wine is considered somewhat of a luxury.

The United States does have its own form of luxury standards. Nearly every home, regardless of income, is equipped with a refrigerator and television set. As a nation, however, the United States lags behind other countries in supplying certain services. Many foreign governments, for instance, provide health care to all their citizens. In the United States, much of health care is not government-supported and is very expensive in relation to other goods and services. If not paid by an employer, health insurance can cost a U.S. family $1,000 a month or more.

Transportation, dramatically different in mode and style from one part of the world to another, is another factor that plays a big role in purchasing power and the standard of living. In the United States, where most people use automobiles for transportation, the total cost of the automobile, fuel, parking, and insurance is significant in many family budgets, generally amounting to hundreds of dollars every month. In some parts of the United States and throughout much of the world outside North America, the majority of the population does not own automobiles. That situation may stem from the availability of

The concrete measure of the standard of living is the average per capita income.

Per Capita Income in the United States 1985 to 2001
(in constant 2001 dollars)

Source: U.S. Bureau of the Census, "Total Current Population Survey Per Capita Income," *Current Population Survey*, 2001.

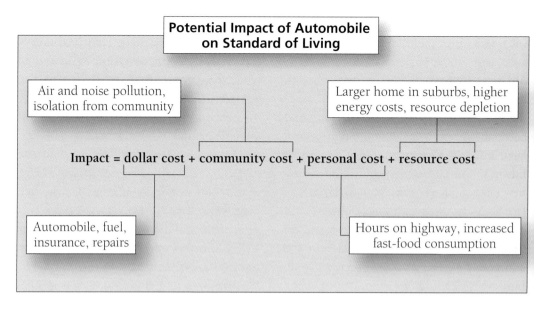

Potential Impact of Automobile on Standard of Living

Air and noise pollution, isolation from community

Larger home in suburbs, higher energy costs, resource depletion

Impact = dollar cost + community cost + personal cost + resource cost

Automobile, fuel, insurance, repairs

Hours on highway, increased fast-food consumption

The effect of an item on one's standard of living, in this example a car, takes a number of potentially negative factors into account.

excellent public transportation, from a lack of purchasing power necessary to own automobiles, or from some people's preference to spend money on other things.

The effect of automobiles on standard of living extends beyond their expense. The quality of air, whether it is clean or polluted, and the ambient environment, whether it is noisy or quiet, figure appreciably in everyday existence. The ways in which a freeway system cuts through a community, separating one segment from another, creating barriers, unsightliness, or noise pollution, affects community life and even home values. The lifestyle the automobile engenders, more hours on the highway, increasing numbers of fast-food meals, and larger homes in the suburbs, can result in energy and resource depletion and a rising number of life-threatening risk factors, all of which come together to determine, in part, the standard of living.

Why do people voluntarily choose certain lifestyles, riding in unsafe, air-polluting automobiles and eating poor-quality food that also clogs their arteries? The answer lies in aspirations, the final factor in the standard of living equation. Some believe that aspiration, or a desire for goods, is inherent in humankind, a natural part of the human condition. Counterarguments point to times throughout history when people voluntarily traveled light, avoiding the accumulation of possessions. In the United States, the

American Dream did not capture the imagination of the country until the 1920s. Goods that were previously scarce became abundant and Americans grew enthusiastic about consumption. Young people turned their backs on the thrifty ways of their immigrant and pioneer ancestors, espousing a new kind of waste and excess that is minimal by today's standards but was bold in its day.

Soon Americans were defining themselves by what they owned and shaping their aspirations by what their neighbors owned. Research in the 1920s showed that regardless of social class or economic status, young Americans agreed that there was a desirable standard of living to which they aspired. None, however, believed they could reach it. For nearly everyone, yearnings exceeded earnings, and for the first time, Americans complained publicly about what they could not afford. Thus the country began its quest for the ever-elusive and ever-escalating higher standard of living.

Further Reading

Brooks, David. *Bobos in Paradise: The New Upper Class and How They Got There.* Waterville, Maine: Thorndike Press, 2001.

Glickman, Lawrence B., ed. *Consumer Society in American History: A Reader.* Ithaca, N.Y.: Cornell University Press, 1999.

Marchand, Roland. *Advertising the American Dream: Making Way for Modernity, 1920–1940.* Berkeley: University of California Press, 1985.

—*Karen Ehrle*

Standard Oil

Although the combustible properties of oil had been known since ancient times, until the nineteenth century oil collection could be done only in areas where the oil percolated to the surface naturally. In 1859 Col. Edwin Drake and William A. Smith used a new method, drilling, to bring oil to the surface at Oil Creek in Titusville, Pennsylvania. The discovery triggered an oil rush as fortune seekers hurried to the site to buy land and construct oil derricks. The boom-and-bust cycle of the oil industry had begun.

Standard Oil was one of the first big industrial monopolies in the United States. Its business practices triggered demands for antitrust legislation. Standard Oil, and the control it held over the oil industry, was the work of one man—John D. Rockefeller.

The Founding of Standard Oil

Cleveland, Ohio, the largest railroad hub close to the oil fields of Pennsylvania, became a major refining center for the booming oil industry. In 1863 Rockefeller and his partner, Maurice B. Clark, entered the oil business as refiners. Together with Samuel Andrews, who had some refining experience, they built and operated an oil refinery under the company name of Andrews, Clark & Company. In 1865 the partners, now five in number, disagreed about the management of their business affairs and decided to sell the refinery to whichever partner bid the highest. Rockefeller was a high bidder at $72,500; he and Andrews then formed Rockefeller & Andrews. The company was reorganized in 1870 into the Standard Oil Company. Rockefeller's partners in Standard included his brother William, Andrews, and Henry M. Flagler.

The price of oil fluctuated wildly in the early days of the oil industry. For the first few years, petroleum was fetching $20 a barrel. As oil production increased, the price fell to 10 cents a barrel in 1866, rose to $7 in 1868, and then fell to less than $4 a barrel in 1870.

Refineries had trouble making a profit in an environment of massive price fluctuation—their costs for refining oil remained stable, while the amount they paid for the oil rose and fell constantly. Rockefeller realized that the best way to control the price of oil was to own or control all of the refineries, along with the means of moving the oil to the refineries—the railroads.

Standard was able to gain influence over the railroads by buying, together with other refiners, a small company, the South Improvement Company (SIC). Rockefeller managed to convince the railroads that the SIC was actually a much larger alliance than it was. The railroads gave SIC favorable shipping rates while Rockefeller used his

See also:
Monopoly; Price Fixing; Rockefeller, John D.; Sherman Antitrust Act; Texaco.

Standard Oil

1863
John D. Rockefeller, Samuel Andrews, and Maurice B. Clark form Andrews, Clark & Company.

1865
Rockefeller buys Andrews, Clark & Company for $72,500.

1870
The firm Rockefeller & Andrews is reorganized into Standard Oil Company.

1872
National Refiners Association owns 80 percent of American refineries.

1879
Ohio court rules that Standard Oil used unfair means to build a monopoly.

1904
Ida Tarbell publishes *History of the Standard Oil Company.*

1911
Standard Oil found to be in violation of the 1890 Sherman Antitrust Act.

John D. Rockefeller, Sr., walking with his son John D. Rockefeller, Jr., in 1915.

From the start, Rockefeller had gained control of the industry by being more ruthless, more farsighted, and more focused on costs and efficiency than anyone else. What Rockefeller could not get through persuasion, he got through bribery, sabotage, and underhanded business dealings. Even when railroad rates to nonassociation members were doubled, prompting a congressional investigation, Standard did not back down in its demands for preferential rates. Thousands of separate individuals owned thousands of small oil fields. Such fragmentation worked against uniting to restrict production. These small producers could not gain enough leverage over the National Refiners Association to raise the rates they were paid for oil.

As the consolidation process continued, Standard came under increasing scrutiny from various state governments. Standard's deals with the railroads were forcing up the price not only of petroleum products, but also of shipping other goods, including food. These price increases were causing hardships and added to costs in other industries. In 1879 Standard and Rockefeller lost a court battle in Ohio, which declared that Standard had used unfair means to build a monopoly. Rockefeller had to try a new strategy to maintain the monopoly.

The Standard Trust

Between 1879 and 1882 Rockefeller merged his various oil businesses into the Standard Trust, a vehicle by which he could coordinate all oil production, refining, transportation, and distribution. The shareholders of the corporations in the trust would hand their shares to nine trustees and would be issued trust certificates in exchange, entitling them to a share of the trust's profits (dividends). The trust allowed the 40 companies controlled by Rockefeller and his partners to invest in each other, a completely new concept. The trust controlled 90 percent of the refining capacity of the United States, and produced only what was necessary to keep prices constant. Other trusts, such as the Sugar Trust, Steel Trust,

influence over the railroads to raise shipping rates for everyone else.

Once in control of the distribution network, Standard was able to cut its kerosene prices, force out the competition in the Cleveland area, drive other refineries into bankruptcy, and then buy them out. By 1872 Standard Oil had purchased nearly all the refineries in Cleveland plus two refineries in the New York City area. A full 80 percent of all American refineries belonged to the National Refiners Association, whose president was John D. Rockefeller. Standard could now dictate not only the price it paid drillers for oil but also the price of the refined product.

and Tobacco Trust, soon formed, emulating Rockefeller's strategy, although most of these trusts ultimately failed.

The power and wealth of the Standard Trust was enormous. In 1910 Rockefeller's net worth was equal to nearly 2.5 percent of the entire U.S. economy, the equivalent of nearly $250 billion in 2001.

Political pressure on all the trusts began to grow through the 1880s. Legislatures worried about loss of power, while some journalists, who came to be known as muckrakers, began to expose the business practices used by the trusts. In 1881 *Atlantic Monthly* ran an article, written by the financial editor of the *Chicago Tribune*, Henry Demarest Lloyd,

So long as railroads can be persuaded to interfere with independent pipelines, to refuse oil freight, to refuse loading facilities, lest they disturb their relations with the Standard Oil Company, it is idle to talk about investigations, or antitrust legislation or application of the Sherman law. So long as the Standard Oil Company can control transportation as it does today, it will remain master of the oil industry and the people of the United States will pay for their indifference and folly.

—Ida Tarbell, *History of the Standard Oil Company,* 1904

criticizing Standard Oil and the emerging trust structure and exposing the growth practices of corporate giants responsible to none but themselves. In the case of Standard, he alleged that Rockefeller, in his efforts to influence the Pennsylvania legal climate, did "everything to the legislators except refine

In this 1888 cartoon entitled "A Monopoly That Requires Crushing," a small company, Tide Water Pipe Line, is seen confronting Standard Oil.

A Standard Oil company refinery in New York in 1942.

them." Ida M. Tarbell, a well-known journalist, followed with the detailed expose *History of the Standard Oil Company* (1904).

The pressure of the muckrakers was greatly responsible for Standard's being dragged before the courts in 1911 and found to be in violation of the 1890 Sherman Antitrust Act. Standard was declared to be an illegal monopoly and ordered broken up into 33 separate entities. These included Standard Oil of New Jersey (now Exxon), Standard Oil of New York (now Mobil), Standard Oil of Ohio (Sohio), Standard Oil of Indiana (now Amoco, part of BP), Standard Oil of California (which became Socal, and is now Chevron), Continental Oil (Conoco), and Atlantic Oil (ARCO).

In her book, Tarbell wrote that concentrations of wealth were just as threatening to liberty as concentrations of political power. Standard Oil, the ancestor of the modern transnational corporation, was, in her view, a real danger to individual initiative and a source of "moral degradation." Many in government agreed, arguing that by making small-scale business impossible, trusts undermined the foundation of liberty. These arguments were used to urge the breakup of Standard, and they are similar to arguments

later used to advocate the breakup of other monopolies, including AT&T.

The dismantling of Standard opened the market for new competitors like Texaco and Gulf. It also paved the way for the development of new petroleum products; one of the weaknesses of a monopoly is that it does not support innovation. The breakup of Standard returned the market to the days of wild fluctuations in the price of oil. In 1935 the Interstate Oil Compact, an oil cartel sanctioned by Congress, was established to keep oil prices constant by matching oil supply to oil demand.

The end of Standard's monopoly did not end Rockefeller's empire. In an ironic twist, many of the smaller companies that emerged from Standard have rejoined. Chevron acquired Gulf in 1984, in what was then the largest corporate merger in U.S. history. Then Exxon merged with Mobil to form a company twice as big as its nearest rival—BP Amoco, which also consists of two former Standard Oil companies (Amoco and Sohio). In 2001 Chevron bought Texaco to create the fifth largest oil company in the world. The three biggest oil companies, all made up of former Standard oil companies, now control almost as much of the market as did Rockefeller.

Further Reading

Economides, Michael, and Ronald Oilgney. *The Color of Oil: The History, the Money, and the Politics of the World's Biggest Business.* Lanham, Md.: Lone Star Books, 2000.

Henderson, Wayne, and Scott Benjamin. *Standard Oil: The First 125 Years.* St. Paul, Minn.: MBI Publishing, 1996.

Hidy, Ralph, and George S. Gibb. *History of Standard Oil Company: New Jersey.* Manchester, N.H.: Ayer Company Publishing, 1987.

Montague, Gilbert Holland. *The Rise and Progress of the Standard Oil Company.* 1904. Reprint, New York: Arno Press, 1973.

Tarbell, Ida. *History of the Standard Oil Company.* 1904. Reprint, Mineola, N.Y.: Dover Publications, 2003.

White, Gerald T. *Formative Years in the Far West: History of the Standard Oil Company and Predecessors Through 1919.* Manchester, N.H.: Ayer Company Publishing, 1976.

—*Lisa Magloff*

Starbucks

Legend has it that the coffee bean was discovered sometime around 850 C.E. by an Ethiopian goatherd named Kaldi, who noticed that his goats were friskier after nibbling on the red berries of a local shrub. Kaldi ate a few berries himself and began to feel happier about life. Fast forward a thousand years to a Seattle coffee roaster that has turned quality coffee into a global caffeine empire.

In Seattle, small, funky coffeehouses have long been popular hangouts. Starbucks Coffee, Tea and Spice roasted its first coffee in 1971. The store, named after the coffee-drinking first mate in Herman Melville's *Moby-Dick*, was the vision of three friends—Jerry Baldwin, Zev Siegel, and Gordon Bowker—who shared a common passion for fine coffee and tea. The trio aimed to provide only the finest-quality beans, roasted the beans themselves, and expanded their small stall in Pike Place Market into three more coffeehouses over the next 10 years.

In 1981 Howard Schultz, vice president of Swedish kitchen equipment manufacturer Hammarplast, noticed that a small business in Washington state was ordering an unusually large number of specialty espresso makers. Curious, Schultz traveled to Seattle to learn more about Starbucks; he was entranced, both with the high-quality coffee and with the hip coffee culture. He wanted to be a part of that culture. "On the five-hour plane trip back to New York the next day, I couldn't stop thinking about Starbucks," Schultz writes in his 1997 autobiography. "It was like a shining jewel. I took one sip of the watery airline coffee and pushed it away. Reaching into my briefcase, I pulled out the bag of Sumatra beans, opened the top, and sniffed. . . . By the time I landed at Kennedy Airport, I knew in my heart that this was it."

Schultz met with Baldwin, Siegel, and Bowker and tried to convince them that Starbucks should expand across the country. The trio did not share Schultz's vision of a national empire of coffee roasters, but his persistence paid off. In September 1982 Schultz was hired to head marketing for Starbucks and to oversee the four Seattle stores.

Following a trip to Italy, Schultz had another coffee-inspired epiphany and left Starbucks to open a string of specialty coffee stores in Seattle modeled after a typical Italian espresso bar. Schultz easily raised $400,000 in seed capital (including backing from his former Starbucks partners) and by the end of 1986 he had $1.25 million in equity. The following year, Schultz purchased Starbucks for $4 million and began to implement his vision for the company.

Ordering a tall, skinny, half-caff, hazelnut cappuccino in most U.S. coffee shops in 1987 would probably have resulted in nothing more than a puzzled look. By 1997 Starbucks had opened 1,270 outlets and had introduced America to European-style coffee. Soon even fast-food restaurants were offering the option of a latte or cappuccino with burgers and fries. In 2001 Starbucks

See also:
Globalization.

Starbucks

1971
Starbucks Coffee, Tea and Spice opens in Seattle.

1981
Howard Schultz, vice president of Hammarplast, visits Starbucks.

1982
Schultz hired to head marketing for Starbucks and oversee its four Seattle stores.

1987
Schultz buys Starbucks for $4 million.

1997
Starbucks operates 1,270 outlets.

2001
Starbucks operates 4,000 outlets.

had 4,000 outlets brewing identical caffe lattes in stores from Los Angeles to London and Saudi Arabia. Almost every day a new Starbucks opens somewhere in the world. Starbucks has become the official coffee of United Airlines, Chicago's Wrigley Field, and a host of other institutions.

To spread the coffee culture, Starbucks also began cobranding its product and logo with other products. Breyer's now offers six flavors of Starbucks ice cream, Seattle-based Redhook brewery sells a Double Black Stout brewed with Starbucks coffee, and PepsiCo distributes a bottled version of Starbucks iced frappuccino to grocery stores. Starbucks has begun offering book selections in conjunction with Oprah Winfrey, as well as compilation CDs of music to drink your coffee by.

Starbucks takes a cookie-cutter approach to brewing the perfect latte. An obsession with customer service is imprinted on new employees in mandatory *barista* (coffee brewer) training sessions that turn teenagers into managers of $800,000-a-year cafes. The teenagers remain faithful, in part because of the company's progressive practices. Annual employee turnover at Starbucks is just 60 percent—compared with 140 percent in the fast-food industry as a whole. Starbucks offers stock options and medical insurance to every employee, even part-timers, as well as basic wages considerably higher than the food-service average. Consumers remain faithful, too. Starbucks serves more than 14 million customers a week, with the average customer visiting a Starbucks 18 times a month.

As markets become inundated with Starbucks outlets, the sight of a Starbucks on every corner has bred some backlash. In some areas, so many new stores open that they cannibalize the sales of existing stores. The company has been accused of encouraging such saturation to drive out smaller competition. Others maintain that quality has been sacrificed to growth, and that Starbucks should be purchasing more beans from small, struggling growers than from large conglomerates. In the

Starbucks courted controversy in 2000 when it opened a franchise in the Forbidden City in Beijing, China. Local media protested the opening of an American franchise in such a culturally and historically important area.

The year 2001 found Howard Schultz, left, chairman of Starbucks, and Starbucks Japan CEO Yuji Tsunoda toasting the listing of Starbucks Japan on the Nasdaq Japan market, the first overseas listing for the U.S.–based coffee chain.

Pacific Northwest, the home of coffeehouse culture, bumper stickers can be seen that read, "Friends Don't Let Friends Go To Starbucks," while small towns like Katonah, New York, have fought to keep the chain out of their quaint main streets. However, by popularizing coffee culture, Starbucks has enabled a whole range of coffee shops and roasters to find a wider market.

With the rise of the Internet, Starbucks began to link the hipness of the Internet culture with the hipness of the relaxed coffeehouse culture. Ninety percent of Starbucks customers are also heavy Internet users, and the stores are popular spots for business meetings. The company plans to install high-capacity phone lines and wireless transmitters in 2,100 of its North American stores. In addition, Starbucks has launched a new chain, Circadia Coffee House, which provides Internet access from each table and well-worn couch. Circadia also sells foccacia, espresso fondue, and floppy disks, and rents laptops and private rooms.

What started out as a labor of love to brew the perfect cup of coffee has become a coffeehouse empire. Although coffee purists, who prefer their brew from small, neighborhood coffeehouses, are infuriated, Starbucks continues to serve an appreciative clientele.

Further Reading

Navarro, Peter. *It's Raining in Brazil, Buy Starbucks.* New York: McGraw-Hill, 2001.

Pendergrast, Mark. *Uncommon Grounds: The History of Coffee and How it Transformed Our World.* Collingdale, Pa.: DIANE Publishing, 2002.

Schultz, Howard. *Pour Your Heart into It: How Starbucks Built a Company One Cup at a Time.* Collingdale, Pa.: DIANE Publishing, 2000.

—*Lisa Magloff*

Stewart, Martha

1941–
Founder, Martha Stewart Omnimedia

Martha Stewart gained widespread recognition in 1982 with the publication of *Entertaining*, her highly successful guide for hosts and hostesses. Since then she has built a multi-million-dollar media empire that reaches more than 88 million people each month. Stewart's persona, her products, and her advocacy for an elegant, picture-perfect American lifestyle have made her familiar to an international audience.

On the surface, appearing on television screens and in books, magazines, videos, and Web sites, Martha Stewart conveys an image of poise, relaxation, and elegance. Behind the smiling face resides a power-house of energy, an exacting taskmaster who devotes 20 hours a day to her business activity—a regimen made possible, Stewart says, by her need for little sleep.

Born Martha Kostyra in 1941, she grew up in Nutley, New Jersey, the daughter of Polish Americans for whom the Great Depression was a recent memory. Her mother was a teacher and homemaker, her father a pharmaceutical salesman; her parents gardened, canned, cooked, and sewed, not for pleasure but because frugality was necessary to provide for their four children.

Mr. and Mrs. Kostyra introduced their children to home skills. Martha remembers her father teaching her to garden when she was three years old. Mrs. Kostyra involved Martha in tasks of homemaking, and neighbors with special skills taught her to bake pies and cakes. Although she learned much from these childhood experiences, Stewart vowed she would have a better life than that of her parents—certainly better than her mother's, which Stewart remembers as a life of hard work for little reward.

Her upbringing also endowed Martha with a confident, independent spirit, one she expressed in her yearbook quotation, "I do as I please and I do it with ease." A straight-A student in high school, Martha attended Barnard College on a scholarship. Initially setting out to be a teacher, she switched majors twice, first to chemistry, then to art and architectural history, the field in which she earned her degree.

In 1960 Martha met Andy Stewart, a Yale law student, and they married the next year. In the early years of her marriage and while she completed her studies at Barnard, Stewart supported herself by modeling in New York City, working in promotions for companies including Breck and Clairol. After graduation she moved from modeling to finance, taking a job as a stockbroker on Wall Street, an ideal environment in which to develop her sales skills and to feed her appetite for advancement.

After the birth of their one child, Alexis, the Stewarts purchased a century-old country house in Westport, Connecticut, where Stewart found new outlets for her energy. She had by then developed an array of competencies in areas ranging from homemaking to art appreciation, from finance to personal appearance. In her first private venture she put these talents to use in a catering business she operated from the basement of her

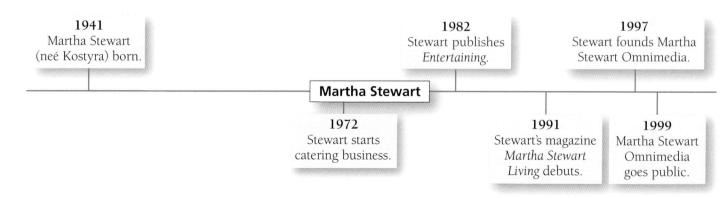

1941
Martha Stewart (neé Kostyra) born.

1982
Stewart publishes *Entertaining*.

1997
Stewart founds Martha Stewart Omnimedia.

Martha Stewart

1972
Stewart starts catering business.

1991
Stewart's magazine *Martha Stewart Living* debuts.

1999
Martha Stewart Omnimedia goes public.

Martha Stewart rings the opening bell at the New York Stock Exchange in 1999.

home. She soon opened a local cooperative shop as well, where she and her neighbors could sell their creations.

In 1979 the style and beauty of one of Stewart's catered events impressed the president of Crown Publishing, and he asked her to write a book. She wrote *Entertaining*, a sumptuous guide for hosts and hostesses.

Appearing first in 1982, it sold more than 500,000 copies and reached its thirtieth edition by 2001. The book launched a career that grew into a business empire. To Stewart's growing audience, the time seemed ripe for rekindling a sense of respect and appreciation for domestic skills and experience. Feminism and affluence created by economic expansion had freed a growing number of women from obligatory housework, and in this context Stewart portrayed the home in a positive light. Her views implied a new status for homemakers, suggesting, in fact, that they might elevate their everyday work to an elite art form.

The success of *Entertaining* positioned Stewart to develop the flagship of her enterprise, the *Martha Stewart Living* magazine. Time Warner introduced this periodical to an enthusiastic public in 1991 and circulation soon reached 1.3 million. The subsequent history of the magazine illustrates Stewart's focused, driving spirit. Time Warner owned the magazine, with Stewart as its highly paid editor. However, she lacked rights to the magazine's contents, which she wanted for use in other ventures. When she and Time Warner could not come to agreement on her proposed initiatives, Stewart set out to buy the magazine. To raise the necessary capital (she reportedly paid $75 million), Stewart expanded a royalties agreement she had entered into with Kmart retailers in 1987.

Kmart approved an expanded role for Martha Stewart merchandise in its bed and bath departments and other retail areas.

The strength of this new arrangement with Kmart enabled Stewart to buy her independence from Time Warner in 1997 and to establish Martha Stewart Omnimedia. Omnimedia publishes the *Martha Stewart Living* magazine and more than a dozen best-selling books; it also produces instructional videos and a nationally syndicated television series. In 1998 Stewart earned $5 million in pay and bonuses from Omnimedia. Omnimedia raised $149 million in 1999 on its initial public offering on the stock market. Stewart's stock was valued at nearly $1 billion in 2000. Stewart emerged as a media celebrity, making regular guest appearances on major network television shows, commanding a reported $10,000 for lectures, and charging $900 per person for Martha Stewart home seminars.

Time listed Stewart as one of "America's 25 Most Influential People" in June 1996, and *Fortune* magazine named her to its list of the "50 Most Powerful Women" in October 1998. The *Martha Stewart Living* television show has received a number of Emmy awards.

In 2002 Stewart's image was tarnished by accusations that she had engaged in illegal insider trading with the sale of stock she held in ImClone. The bad publicity from the investigation hurt Omnimedia, which posted its first loss in the fourth quarter of 2002. Stewart was indicted on charges of securities fraud, conspiracy, and obstruction of justice in June 2003; she declared her innocence but resigned her position as CEO and chair of Omnimedia.

Martha Stewart: A "Perfect" Feminist?

Even before accusations of illegal stock trading were leveled against her in 2002, few public figures produced as intense a response as Martha Stewart. It is a potent mixture of admiration and antipathy.

In a seeming rebuke to feminism, which regarded housework as drudgery weighing women down, Stewart's persona has been that of the perfect hostess—emphasis on "perfect." While feminists urged women to get out of the kitchen, Stewart has used her kitchen to conquer the world, turning a small catering business into a billion-dollar conglomerate. She appears to be the woman who not only has everything but also does everything better than anyone. Perhaps this is why harried modern women took vicarious pleasure in her legal troubles, or in rumors of Stewart's strained relationship with her daughter and of browbeating of her staff—evidence, perhaps, that perfection has its price.

Yet envy is not enough to explain the response that the mere mention of Stewart's name can arouse. Such fervor suggests a more complex reaction, inspired not merely by her success but also by the intimate arena in which she has achieved it. Stewart reaffirms the value and pleasures of what were once called the domestic arts: the countless small efforts that make a house into a home. In doing so, she highlights what is lost in typical two-income households, when no one has the time to fit everyday graciousness into an already packed schedule. After three decades of a brand of feminism that saw little value in "women's work," Stewart's highly profitable domesticity, feminist in its own right, evokes a peculiar mixture of guilt and longing in her viewers.

—*Colleen Sullivan*

Further Reading

Brady, Diane. "Martha, Inc." *BusinessWeek*, January 17, 2000.

Byron, Christopher. *Martha Inc.: The Incredible Story of Martha Stewart Living Omnimedia.* Hoboken, N.J.: John Wiley & Sons, 2002.

Stewart, Martha. *Entertaining.* New York: Crown Publishing, 1998.

———. *The Wedding Planner.* New York: Crown Publishing, 1988.

—*Karen Ehrle*

Stocks and Bonds

The financial markets have become prominent in ongoing news stories; watching television or reading the newspaper almost invariably brings a story on stocks and bonds to our attention. This popularity is attributable in large part to the lengthy bull market (a period of rising stock prices) that saw gains of 20 percent per year from 1995 to 1999, followed by the decline that led to a bear market (decreasing prices) in 2000 and 2001. Interest in financial securities has increased substantially since the mid-1970s as more Americans have gained access and exposure to the market through mutual funds, 401(k) and 403(b) retirement plans, and Individual Retirement Accounts (IRAs). In 1999 the Investment Company Institute and the Securities Industry Association estimated that 48 percent of U.S. households owned stock, up from just 19 percent in 1983.

Although the surge in participation in financial markets is a relatively recent phenomenon, the roots of today's financial markets can be traced to the early 1790s. At that time, the U.S. government began issuing debt (bonds) to pay the debts it had incurred in fighting the Revolutionary War, and it sold 10 million shares of stock to finance the creation of the first U.S. bank. More banks followed, and investors became more interested in investing in stocks and bonds. This increase in demand for financial securities spurred transportation and manufacturing companies to issue their own stock. The U.S. economy has grown through the issuance of debt and equity (stock) by businesses and the purchase of those financial instruments by investors. For more than 200 years, U.S. businesses have benefited from access to one of the most developed capital markets in the world.

Since the 1970s the global financial market has been changing dramatically.

Prior to 1970 the U.S. stock and bond market made up about 65 percent of all financial securities available in the world. In 2001 the U.S. stock and bond market made up less than 50 percent of all securities available worldwide. This shift in the markets has occurred because many less-developed countries are growing quickly and are using debt and equity to fund economic growth.

Stock and Bond Basics

Businesses require capital (money) to grow—to develop new products, build new plants, expand internationally, and invest in technology. Owners of small businesses may choose to use their own savings to start or maintain their business, or they may seek a loan from a bank. Large businesses, corporations like Wal-Mart, General Motors, and Coca-Cola, require large amounts of capital from a variety of sources to fund their growth. Rather than borrowing great sums of money from banks, large businesses often enter capital markets directly by selling stocks or bonds to individual investors.

Stocks and bonds differ fundamentally. Common stock represents ownership of a company. If an investor owns 100 shares of Coca-Cola, he or she owns a minuscule piece of that company and has the right to vote on important issues at the company's annual meeting. With this ownership comes a certain amount of risk because stockholders are not guaranteed a return on their investment. Some companies, for instance, Coca-Cola, distribute a portion of their earnings each year to shareholders in the

See also:
Day Trading; Finance, Personal; Nasdaq; New York Stock Exchange; Savings and Investment Options.

Stocks and Bonds: Risk and Returns 1996 to 2000		
Asset classes	Average annual return	Standard deviation (risk)
Large-company stocks	13.0%	20.2%
Long-term corporate bonds	6.0%	8.7%
Long-term government bonds	5.7%	9.4%
U.S. Treasury bills	3.9%	3.2%

Note: During this period inflation averaged 3.2% per year.
Source: Stocks, Bonds, Bills and Inflation 2001 Yearbook, Ibbotson Associates, Inc., Chicago.

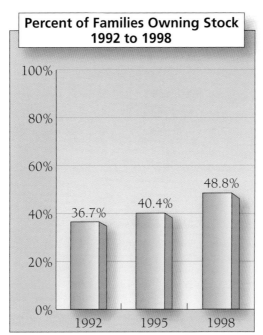

Percent of Families Owning Stock 1992 to 1998

- 1992: 36.7%
- 1995: 40.4%
- 1998: 48.8%

The 1990s witnessed a steady increase in families owning stock.

Source: U.S. Bureau of the Census, *Statistical Abstracts of the United States,* Washington, D.C., Government Printing Office, 2002.

form of dividends. Other companies, including Microsoft, have not traditionally paid annual dividends. Many investors buy stock regardless of dividends because they believe that the value of the company will increase, thereby increasing the value of the individual shares.

Bondholders, on the other hand, are not company owners. A bond is a loan: the individual who buys the bond lends a certain amount of money, called the principal, to the company that issues the bond. Bondholders do not have the opportunity to vote on issues facing the firm because they do not own a piece of the company. They have simply lent capital to the firm, and they receive periodic interest payments in exchange for that loan.

Bond interest payments, unlike stock dividends, are guaranteed. Investment in bonds is, accordingly, less risky than stock investments. Bonds issued by corporations like GM and Wal-Mart are referred to as long-term corporate bonds while bonds issued by the U.S. government are referred to as long-term government bonds. When a firm or government issues a long-term bond, the intention is to borrow money for 10 to 30 years. The U.S. government also issues Treasury bills (T-bills) to borrow money for short periods, usually less than one year.

Risk and Return

If stocks are more risky than bonds, what induces investors to buy stocks? In general, risk and reward go hand in hand. Stock investors, who are willing to bear more risk, generally receive a higher return than bondholders, who wish to bear less risk. Average annual historical returns on stocks and bonds are shown in the table below. The average annual return on stocks of large companies (Coca-Cola and Microsoft, for example) is much larger than the average annual return on bonds. The difference between the returns is 7 percent. That difference is referred to as a risk premium, which measures the extra reward that investors may earn for bearing the additional risk associated with investing in common stock.

The risk of each asset class is measured by the standard deviation. Both the average return on large-company stocks and the standard deviation risk of large-company stocks are more than twice as high as the respective numbers for long-term corporate bonds. As the table to the left illustrates, risk and return generally move in the same direction. The only exception is the long-term government bonds; corporate bonds provide a slightly higher return than government bonds but have slightly less risk.

The table also illustrates that the return on T-bills is only marginally higher than inflation. As inflation erodes the purchasing power of money, investors who invest large sums in low-risk T-bills do not enjoy much

Total Returns of Stocks, Treasury Bills, and Bonds 1950 to 1999
(average annual percent change)

	Stocks	Treasury bills	10-year bonds
1950 to 1959	19.28	2.02	0.73
1960 to 1969	7.78	4.06	2.42
1970 to 1979	5.82	6.42	5.84
1980 to 1989	17.54	9.21	13.06
1990 to 1999	18.17	5.01	7.96

Source: U.S. Bureau of the Census, *Statistical Abstracts of the United States,* Washington, D.C., Government Printing Office, 2002.

In 2000 a trader in the Nasdaq 100 Stock futures pit at the Chicago Mercantile Exchange signals a trade.

increase in purchasing power. To enjoy increased purchasing power through time without bearing the risk of an investment portfolio containing only common stock, investors must diversify their portfolio across asset classes, allocating money to stocks, long-term bonds, and T-bills. Furthermore, studies show that investors should have a portion of their portfolio invested in international securities. The exact allocation of money across asset classes depends on the individual investor's risk tolerance, age, financial goals, and constraints.

Issuance and Trading

When a company wishes to sell equity or borrow money by issuing bonds, the firm typically employs an investment banker, also known as an underwriter, to assist with the issuance process. Security issuance is an involved process because the companies that wish to issue securities must disclose a

A Capital Cities/ABC shareholder speaks out against the company's proposed merger with the Walt Disney Company at a shareholders' meeting in 1996.

significant amount of information about their company to potential investors. This information is assembled in a prospectus, a document that must be approved by the Securities and Exchange Commission (SEC). The SEC was created by Congress in 1934 to regulate securities trading and protect the interests of current and potential investors. The prospectus contains information about the company's financial prospects and business operations. Before investing in any securities, investors should study the prospectus carefully.

When a company issues stocks and bonds and subsequently receives the proceeds

from the sale of the stocks or bonds, the transaction is referred to as a primary market transaction. After the primary market transaction, investors can trade securities among themselves through the secondary market. The firm itself does not receive any money from secondary market transactions. In 2001 the average trading volume on the New York Stock Exchange (NYSE), which is a secondary market, was more than 1.2 billion shares, or $42 billion, per day. The largest trading day was September 17, 2001, when 2.4 billion shares were traded. These recent volume numbers are even more impressive considering that prior to

1960, volume averaged less than 3 million shares per day.

The bond market is small compared with the equity market. In 2001 bond trading averaged just under $10 million per day on the NYSE. For both stocks and bonds, the majority of this volume originates in secondary market transactions (investors trading with each other). Very few transactions involve the sale of new stock or bonds by a firm.

To buy bonds or individual shares of stock, investors typically must have an account with a financial institution, usually a brokerage firm that owns a seat on a U.S. securities exchange. Brokerage firms that own one or more seats on an exchange have trading privileges on that exchange and can buy and sell securities on the floor of the exchange. When an investor wishes to buy or sell, he or she places an order with a broker. The order is entered into the brokerage firm's computer system, travels to company headquarters, and enters the exchange's vast computer network. The order then proceeds to the trading floor where it is executed, and confirmation of the trade is sent to the investor. On average, less than 22 seconds are needed to process a trade because of the advanced technology that has been put in place by the stock exchanges. The NYSE alone has spent more than $2 billion on computer technology.

Technology and the Amateur Investor

The increased use of technology to facilitate stock trading has coincided with the growth of the Internet as a tool of commerce. In the mid-1990s several online discount brokers arrived on the trading scene, offering low-cost stock trades. Full-service brokers provide investment advice combined with trading; discount brokers only execute trades. The arrival of online discount brokers also coincided with the beginning of an incredible up-trend in the stock market. From 1995 to 1999, U.S. stocks returned more than 20 percent per year; prior to that run, the market had had no more than two years of back-to-back 20 percent increases.

This five-year period of incredible returns gave many investors unfounded confidence in their stock selection abilities and enticed them into trading for themselves through online discount brokers. Some investors became so interested in the market that they began day trading. Day trading goes against the traditional theory of long-term investing because it involves buying shares of stock and holding them only long enough to earn a quick profit. Some day traders earned large sums; others lost large sums when they bought stocks that decreased in value. By mid-2000 the popularity of day trading had begun to wane as the market started to tumble. The bull market that essentially began in 1982 ended in 2000, when the U.S. stock markets were actually down for the year, a trend that continued in 2001 and 2002.

Money lubricates the gears of the U.S. system of free enterprise, and the stock and bond markets provide an efficient way to transfer money from investors to businesses. The financial markets in the United States are some of the most developed markets in the world and are constantly evolving and changing to meet the needs of businesses as well as individual investors. Although the global capital market has more than $50 trillion invested in stocks, bonds, real estate, and cash, stocks and bonds remain the financial securities held by the vast majority of investors.

Further Reading

Bodie, Zvi, Alex Kane, and Alan J. Marcus. *Essentials of Investments.* New York: McGraw-Hill, 2000.

Brindze, Ruth. *Investing Money: The Facts about Stocks and Bonds.* New York: Harcourt, Brace & World, 1968.

Malkiel, Burton. *A Random Walk down Wall Street.* New York: W. W. Norton, 2002.

Reilly, Frank K., and Edgar A. Norton. *Investments.* Mason, Ohio: South-Western Thomson Learning, 2002.

Siegel, Jeremy. *Stocks for the Long Run.* New York: McGraw-Hill, 2002.

—*Angeline Lavin*

Strategic Planning

Strategic planning is a system used by businesses and other organizations throughout the world. The system uses a long-term time horizon and emphasizes the creation of an appropriate "strategic fit" between an organization and its external environment. George C. Morrisey, a writer and international consultant in strategic planning, divides strategic planning into three main stages: strategic thinking, long-range planning, and tactical planning.

Strategic thinking begins with the development of mission and vision statements as well as a statement of shared values and beliefs. A mission statement identifies a business's purpose. It answers the question "Why does this business exist?" The answer might include identifying the needs the business fulfills for customers (for example, an automobile company fulfills a transportation need), the products and services the organization offers (and will offer) to satisfy those needs, the market that is and will be targeted by the business, and the technology that will be used in fulfilling the needs in question.

Vision statements are another direction-setting tool. They describe a business as it will exist at some time in the future; the statements can powerfully motivate employees. Statements of the shared values and beliefs have also become popular direction-setting tools in the strategic planning process. These statements can help to form the backbone of an organization's culture, guiding people in the decisions they make by limiting alternative possibilities to those that fit within stated values and beliefs. Direction setting carried out in the strategic thinking phase is for the long term, often 10 to 15 years. Accordingly, the direction provided must be general enough to allow for some strategic flexibility, yet specific enough to provide guidance and allow for the development of the requisite competencies within the organization.

The long-range planning stage adds specific detail to the general plan. Two dominant direction setting tools at this stage are long-range objectives and strategy. Long-range objectives often have a time horizon of two to five years; they identify specific results to be accomplished within that period. For instance, a business may have an objective to increase sales to $100 million in five years. Businesses engaged in long-term planning often work with between five and ten objectives of this sort. With too many objectives, a business risks losing focus and initiative by trying to do too much. Too few objectives may create too narrow a focus, making the business less effective. Whatever the number of objectives, they should be directed at helping the business carry out its mission and realize its vision within the constraints identified through its statement of shared values.

To attain their objectives, businesses formulate strategies. Appropriate strategy formulation requires an analysis of the organization's internal and external environments, often referred to as a SWOT

Strategic Planning Process

Development of Mission and Vision Statements
- Identify business purpose
- Identify product need
- Identify market
- Identify needed technology
- View business as it will exist in future

Tactical Planning
- Set short-term (one year) objectives
- Develop action plans

Long Range Planning
- Set two- to five-year objectives
- Develop strategy

(Strengths, Weaknesses, Opportunities, Threats) analysis. A SWOT analysis determines a business's strengths and weaknesses by analyzing the various business units, functional areas, and processes within the organization; opportunities and threats are uncovered by analyzing the external environment. The external environment is often divided into two segments, the operating, or task, environment and the general environment.

In *Competitive Advantage: Creating and Sustaining Superior Performance*, Michael Porter identifies five major sources of competition that should be assessed in the operating environment prior to developing strategy: rival firms in the industry; suppliers of important inputs; buyers of a firm's outputs; new firms that might enter the industry; and makers of substitute products or services. Analysis of the general environment involves consideration of the business's objectives as they might be affected by changes in the economic, technological, social–cultural, and legal–political context. Any strategic response seeks to use the strengths of the business, exploiting opportunities in its environment. It also seeks to steer the business away from threats in its environment and to minimize internal weaknesses. Once the strategy is decided on, action plans are developed for the attainment of each long-term objective.

Tactical planning usually includes the development of short-term (often one year) objectives and action plans. These objectives and actions are often targeted to specific units or positions in a business.

Most strategic planning models include implementation and control stages following the development of the strategic plan. Implementation often requires changes in the organizational structure and reallocation of resources. The control stage provides regular feedback to allow for changes as needed. The implementation and control stages clearly show that strategic planning carries over into management. Accordingly, businesspeople often refer to the entire

Key Strategic Issues
Key Strategic Issues
• Industry in which company will operate
• Existing product lines within industry
• Price and quantity of products
• Targeted customers and markets
• Firm's marketing policies
• Firm's manufacturing policies
• Firm's financial policies

Source: John Leslie Livingstone, and Theodore Grossman, *The Portable MBA in Finance and Accounting,* New York, Wiley, 2002.

process as strategic management rather than strategic planning.

Although strategic planning continues to be popular in the business world, it does have critics. Henry Mintzberg charges that three major fallacies often affect the use of strategic planning. The first fallacy is that of predetermination. Successful strategic planning requires forecasting the future and developing a direction for the organization in light of that forecast. Such forecasts are useful if existing trends continue, but businesses often operate in volatile, unpredictable environments. A strategic plan may cause a business to undervalue new information about these environments if it does not fit well with the predetermined direction. The second fallacy is that of detachment. Most strategic planning models assume a top-down approach in which the major responsibility for planning lies with top managers while implementation is carried out by lower level managers and employees. This separation of plan development from implementation is, according to Mintzberg, similar to trying to separate thinking from doing. At the very least,

SWOT Analysis	
Strengths Weaknesses	Analyze various business units, functional areas and processes within organization
Opportunities Threats	Analyze external environment

Sometimes employees are asked to analyze specific aspects of the business environment—for example, the market or the competition— and make presentations to the rest of the company.

such separation decreases the new learning that occurs as a business carries out its plan. The third fallacy is that of formalization. A formalized process may not be an effective means for developing innovative strategies for organizations. Instead, formalized planning may favor the institutionalization of existing strategies.

Strategic planning has limitations. Using strategic planning does not guarantee business success. However, strategic planning does push managers to consider the long-term effects of decisions made by, and actions of, everyone working in their organizations. Further, it pushes managers to monitor conditions within the organization and in the external environment. Although strategic planning cannot guarantee success, its continued popularity in the business world suggests that its benefits outweigh its drawbacks.

Further Reading

Andrews, Kenneth R. *The Concept of Corporate Strategy.* Homewood, Ill.: Irwin, 1971.

Fry, Fred L., Charles R. Stoner, and Laurence G. Weinzimmer. *Strategic Planning for New and Emerging Businesses.* 2nd ed. Chicago, Ill.: Dearborn Trade, 1999.

Mintzberg, Henry. *The Rise and Fall of Strategic Planning.* New York: The Free Press, 1994.

Morrisey, George L. *Morrisey on Planning: A Guide to Strategic Thinking.* San Francisco: Jossey-Bass Publishers, 1996.

Porter, Michael E. *Competitive Advantage: Creating and Sustaining Superior Performance.* New York: The Free Press, 1985.

—Will Drago

Strikes

Labor strikes are an attempt by workers to improve or protect their working conditions by refusing to work until either their demands are met or a compromise is reached. Strikes are a significant part of labor history in both the United States and around the world. They have been used in an effort to draw attention to the working conditions of the strikers and to put economic pressure on employers to ameliorate those conditions.

The nature of strikes has evolved as economic, political, and demographic conditions have changed. For example, in the early years of the U.S. labor movement, before the rise of organized labor and the institutionalization of unions, many strikes were extremely political in nature, emphasizing fundamental economic and social reforms. The general strike, a tactic infrequently used in the United States, is a massive work stoppage across many industries that often has political as well as economic overtones.

Strikes are not always directed against employers. As early as the 1600s, fishermen, butchers, printers, shoemakers, and other artisans refused to work at one time or another. In 1741 bakers in New York refused to work because of the high prices they had to pay for wheat.

Industrialization

The nature of strikes changed as workers organized into labor unions. After the Civil War, the United States experienced a significant growth in industrialization. The nineteenth century witnessed an important shift in the economic base and demographics of the nation. What was once primarily an agrarian country largely populated by independent farmers, artisans, merchants, and owners of small factories developed into an industrialized nation with an ever-increasing number of workers employed in new industries.

This transformation from independent workers to a labor force increasingly employed in large factories, mines, mills, and railroads, provided the conditions for organized labor to gradually emerge as a

Work Stoppages in the U.S. 1960 to 2000 (in thousands)				
Year	Total work stoppages[1]	Workers involved[2]	Days idle[3]	Percentage of work time lost
1960	222	896	13,260	9%
1965	268	999	15,140	10%
1969	412	1,576	29,397	16%
1970	381	2,468	52,761	29%
1971	298	2,516	35,538	19%
1972	250	975	16,764	9%
1973	317	1,400	16,260	8%
1974	424	1,796	31,809	16%
1975	235	965	17,563	9%
1976	231	1,519	23,962	12%
1977	298	1,212	21,258	10%
1978	219	1,006	23,774	11%
1979	235	1,021	20,409	9%
1980	187	795	20,844	9%
1981	145	729	16,908	7%
1982	96	656	9,061	4%
1983	81	909	17,461	8%
1984	62	376	8,499	4%
1985	54	324	7,079	3%
1986	69	533	11,861	5%
1987	46	174	4,481	2%
1988	40	118	4,381	2%
1989	51	452	16,996	7%
1990	44	185	5,926	2%
1991	40	392	4,584	2%
1992	35	364	3,989	1%
1993	35	182	3,981	1%
1994	45	322	5,020	2%
1995	31	192	5,771	2%
1996	37	273	4,889	2%
1997	29	339	4,497	1%
1998	34	387	5,116	2%
1999	17	73	1,996	1%
2000	39	394	20,419	6%

Note: Excludes work stoppages involving fewer than 1,000 workers and lasting less than one day. Information is based on reports of labor disputes appearing in daily newspapers, trade journals, and other public sources.
[1] Beginning in year indicated. [2] Workers counted more than once if involved in more than one stoppage during the year.
[3] Total number of days of work lost resulting from all stoppages in effect in a year, including those that began in an earlier year.
Source: U.S. Bureau of Labor Statistics, *Work Stoppages Summary*, USDL 01-41, February 9, 2001.

See also:
AFL-CIO; Collective Bargaining; Labor Union; Teamsters Union; United Automobile Workers of America; Working Conditions.

powerful force in the shaping of the nation's political and economic future.

By the early nineteenth century, the process of industrialization was gaining momentum. Artisans were discovering that where once they had been the owners of the means of production—that is, they worked with their own tools in a place of their choice—they were now being displaced by new technologies. The Industrial Revolution altered the economic base of the United States and increasingly forced workers into mills and factories. For example, when mass production of shoes made shoes cheaper, the artisan shoemaker found an increasingly limited market for handmade wares. Weavers, who had worked at looms in their homes for centuries, were gradually replaced by mill workers, many of them women and children.

In 1853 and 1854 approximately 400 strikes were called in the United States. A strike in 1860 by more than 10,000 workers employed in the manufacture of shoes marked the largest labor walkout to that time. Following the Civil War, both the labor movement and the number of strikes grew in response to increased industrialization. However, as population centers swelled, employers found recruiting strikebreakers (sometimes called scabs by striking workers) easier.

Violence and failed strikes led many unions to adopt new strategies. An important change was the transfer of authority to call strikes from the rank-and-file workers to union officials. Nevertheless, the 1870s witnessed a number of strikes that had significant national impact.

During the severe economic depression of 1873, for example, workers resisting wage cuts struck the New England textile industry, anthracite coal mines, and the Pennsylvania Railroad. These strikes occurred despite the threat workers faced of being charged with criminal conspiracy or of being fired and blacklisted (laws had not yet been enacted protecting the rights of workers to organize). Workers, as a result, often kept their organizing efforts hidden from employers.

The Molly Maguires, a secret group of Pennsylvania miners, succeeded in calling a strike in 1875 in response to the harsh living and working conditions of miners at that time. The Pinkerton National Detective Agency, the first nationwide private company of investigators, was hired to infiltrate the organization. Court testimony from Pinkerton agents resulted in the destruction of the Molly Maguires and to the hanging of a number of its members in 1877. The Pinkertons, as they came to be called, were instrumental in breaking many strikes in the nineteenth century.

The Summer of 1877

The year 1877 remains a watershed in the history of labor. One of the nation's rare general strikes began in July when approximately 100,000 railroad workers, joined by workers in other industries as well as the unemployed, stopped rail traffic throughout the East and Midwest and brought the nation to a virtual standstill.

What had begun spontaneously among a group of railroad workers protesting wage reductions in the Martinsburg, West Virginia, yards of the Baltimore & Ohio (B&O), spread to Pittsburgh, St. Louis, and Chicago. The Martinsburg strikers vowed that no trains would leave that city until a 10 percent wage cut was rescinded. When B&O officials asked for state support to quell the strike, the governor sent in the militia. Gunfire was exchanged and a striker was killed.

As more freight trains jammed the Martinsburg yards, the governor asked President Rutherford Hayes for federal troops. After their arrival, the freight trains started rolling, but this was only the beginning of the struggle. In Baltimore, thousands of people in sympathy with the strikers gathered at the National Guard armory. Called out by the governor of Maryland at the behest of the railroad, soldiers started firing on the rock-throwing crowd. By the end of the confrontation, 10 people were dead and many wounded. After passenger cars, the station platform, and a locomotive were set ablaze, 500 federal troops were called in and Baltimore was silenced.

Still the strike spread. In Pittsburgh the Pennsylvania Railroad was struck when a worker refused a dangerous job. Other crew members also refused and the stage was set. The strikers were joined by workers from iron mills, factories, mines, and oil refineries. Two thousand trains were idle. Again troops were called in and more deaths followed.

When the entire Pennsylvania National Guard was called out, strikers blocked the roads. Workers in Pottsville and Reading joined what was taking on the characteristics of a general strike. In Reading, one group of soldiers refused to fire on the workers. Although the leaders of the Order of Railway Conductors, Brotherhood of Locomotive Firemen, and Brotherhood of Engineers did not endorse the strike, momentum was building in support of the workers.

In Chicago, the Workingman's Party called a rally. Thousands participated and demanded that the railroads be nationalized. An armed crowd clashed with police for over two days and more deaths resulted. In St. Louis, workers from a wide range of industries joined railroad strikers. In New York, several thousand gathered at a rally in support of the strikes. What had started as a protest against wage cuts was increasingly taking on political overtones. The strikes made international headlines.

As the summer of 1877 faded, so did the energy of the strikers. The combined strength of the police, militias, and federal troops was no match for the unorganized crowds. By the time the strike ended, 70 members of the Workingman's Party had been arrested, more than 100 strike leaders had been fired, approximately 100 people were dead and 1,000 imprisoned. The railroads did make some concessions and agreed to roll back some wage cuts; they also increased their security.

The Labor Movement at the
Turn of the Twentieth Century

In the 1880s the number of strikes grew from fewer than 500 per year in the early part of the decade to about 1,500 in 1886. Issues included wages, working conditions,

FRANK LESLIE'S ILLUSTRATED WEEKLY

HOMESTEAD TROUBLES.

Vol. LXXV—No. 1932.
Copyright, 1892, by Askell Weekly Co.
All Rights Reserved.

NEW YORK, JULY 14, 1892.

[Price, 10 Cents. $4.00 Yearly.]

THE LABOR TROUBLES AT HOMESTEAD, PENNSYLVANIA—ATTACK OF THE STRIKERS AND THEIR SYMPATHIZERS ON THE SURRENDERED PINKERTON MEN.—Drawn by Miss G. A. Davis, from a Sketch by C. Upham.—[See Page 47.]

work rules, and union recognition. Workers living in the nineteenth and early twentieth centuries were inspired by the new political and economic theorists of the time including Mikhail Bakunin and Karl Marx. The ideals of anarchism and communism, as well as the calls for a redistribution of wealth and nationalization of certain industries, alarmed both Washington and Wall Street.

State and federal troops were called out hundreds of times to subdue labor unrest. In 1892, when Pinkerton guards failed to stop strikers at a Homestead, Pennsylvania, steel

In an 1892 weekly paper, the labor troubles in Pennsylvania are depicted—Pinkerton men attack strikers in an attempt to crush a strike against the Carnegie Steel Company.

The Bisbee Deportation

In the early twentieth century, mines in Arizona produced almost 50 percent of the U.S. supply of copper. Profits were increasing steadily, but miners' wages lagged behind inflation. Miners lived in company-owned housing in company-dominated communities, where they were charged artificially high prices at company stores. The Industrial Workers of the World (IWW, or Wobblies) began organizing miners in Bisbee, Arizona, to fight for better pay and working conditions.

In 1917 the Wobblies demanded a minimum wage based on the quantity of copper produced rather than a flat rate. They also denounced dangerous working practices, for example, detonating dynamite close to workers. Officials from Phelps Dodge, the company that owned the mines, refused to meet with the miners, and, on June 27, 1917, the miners went on strike.

Phelps Dodge complained that the IWW was a treasonous organization, portraying the Wobblies as violent thugs intent on blowing up the mines. In addition to verbally attacking the IWW, the mining companies infiltrated the union with undercover agents to disrupt its proceedings. The local sheriff, Harry C. Wheeler, with the help of Phelps Dodge executives, began deputizing residents and forming a vigilante group. Early in the morning of July 12, 1917, the vigilantes captured Bisbee's telephone and telegraph lines. They rounded up more than 2,000 miners and marched them to a ball field. (Many were neither Wobblies nor strikers.) The miners were given an opportunity to abandon the strike; those who refused, 1,185 in all, were forced to board a train, which took them to New Mexico.

The miners were abandoned in the desert near Hermanas. They were left there, without shelter, for two days until U.S. troops finally rescued them on July 14. In Bisbee, mounted guards patrolled the streets to make sure none of the deportees returned, while many of the miners were detained by the federal government for several months. The strike was broken.

President Woodrow Wilson ordered the Federal Mediation Commission to investigate the incident, and the commission found the mining companies at fault. No action was taken against them, however, either by the federal government or the state of Arizona. About 300 deportees filed civil suits against the El Paso Southwestern Railroad and the copper companies, but these were settled out of court.

mill owned by Andrew Carnegie, the U.S. Army was brought in. The army was also called in to quell the 1894 Pullman strike.

The Pullman strike occurred when George Pullman, inventor of the railroad sleeping car, cut wages by 30 percent but refused to lower prices for food and housing in his company-owned town. When Pullman would not negotiate with the American Railway Union, its president, Eugene Debs, called a strike. Federal troops eventually broke the strike, Debs was imprisoned, and the union defeated.

At the turn of the century American workers were confronted with several struggles. In addition to facing often inhuman working conditions for exploitive wages, they were caught in the sometimes acrimonious debates among labor leaders themselves. Organizations like the Industrial Workers of the World (IWW), whose rallying cry was "one big union," competed with the exclusionary policies of the American Federation of Labor (AFL) for working people's support.

In the early years of the century, the number of strikes remained high, peaking in 1919 when four million workers (one-fifth of the total labor force) struck at some time during the year. In Boston, a walkout by city police was the nation's first strike by public employees; New York saw strikes by garment workers; textile workers and telephone operators went on strike in New England. In Seattle, a general strike brought the city almost to a standstill for five days.

The Great Depression and the New Deal

Over the next decade the number of strikes declined for a variety of reasons. The relationship between labor and management was significantly affected under New Deal programs initiated during the administration of President Franklin D. Roosevelt. In 1934 striking autoworkers, truckers, and longshoremen won concessions from their industries. In 1935 passage of the National Labor Relations Act was hailed as a landmark for labor. The act, also known as the Wagner Act, formally established industrial workers' rights to collective bargaining but ignored workers in other areas including agriculture.

The concept of a state-bestowed right to collective bargaining would have seemed bizarre to the socialists and anarchists who inspired an earlier generation of workers. Some scholars argue that the establishment of work programs, social security, and other apparatus of the welfare state under Roosevelt represented a compromise that averted a radical shift in American politics. Others see those programs as a radicalization in themselves. Following the Great Depression and the New Deal, labor politics became increasingly institutionalized, as labor leaders gained power and authority—often at the expense of rank-and-file workers.

One significant exception to this trend was a six-week strike against General Motors in 1937. Strikers, without the approval of union leaders, adopted a new tactic: the sit-down strike. Workers stopped their labor but remained inside the company's facilities; by taking over the factory, the strikers denied the company the choice of hiring replacement workers. The sit-down strike can also be seen as an attempt by workers to retain control over their working lives without a labor boss as intermediary. The strike's success prompted a series of similar actions before the Supreme Court ruled in 1939 that this kind of labor action was illegal.

New Era for Labor

Because workers gained substantial rights during the 1930s, with employers legally bound to bargain with unions, the tenor of relations between labor and management in the last half of the twentieth century changed dramatically. Written contracts, arbitration, and negotiation became the norm and the overall number of strikes declined.

When strike activity spiked following World War II, antilabor forces succeeded in passing the 1947 Taft–Hartley Act. A thorn in the side of labor ever since, this act curtailed union rights and permitted states to adopt right-to-work laws. These laws allow individuals to work in a unionized workplace without requiring union membership. Although union leaders decried the act as a "slave labor bill," in truth big labor was becoming increasingly indistinguishable from big business. The essential shift in labor–management relations was reflected in labor organizations being content with a bigger piece of the capitalist pie rather than insisting on the political and economic reforms supported by earlier generations of workers.

Striking UPS workers at a rally in 1996.

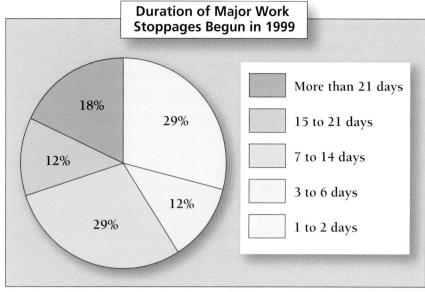

Duration of Major Work Stoppages Begun in 1999

- 29% — 15 to 21 days
- 18% — More than 21 days
- 12% — 3 to 6 days
- 29% — 1 to 2 days
- 12% — 7 to 14 days

Legend:
- More than 21 days
- 15 to 21 days
- 7 to 14 days
- 3 to 6 days
- 1 to 2 days

Source: Bureau of Labor Statistics, http://www.bls.gov/opub/ted/2001/jan/wk3/art02.txt (April 8, 2003).

Although strikes in the private sector were declining, the number of strikes by public employees was on the increase. In 1970 a wildcat strike (a strike not authorized by union leadership) by close to 200,000 postal employees marked the largest walkout of public employees to that date. This 1970 action was also noteworthy because it was taken by public employees (workers employed either by the local, state, or federal government).

The issue of the right of public employees to go on strike reached a crisis in 1981, when negotiations between the Federal Aeronautics Administration and the air traffic controllers' union failed. On August 3, 11,000 air traffic controllers went on strike. When they refused to return to work after an ultimatum from President Ronald Reagan, the strikers were fired and permanently replaced by other workers. In addition, the FAA was banned from rehiring the former workers.

The failure of the air traffic controllers' strike was emblematic of the changes affecting labor in the United States as well as in other nations. A postindustrial, multinational, globalized economy was a new challenge for the working class. The antiunion policies of the Reagan administration brought about close to two decades of diminished labor activity. In 1997, however, the success of a nationwide UPS strike by Teamsters gave organized labor renewed confidence. The closing years of the twentieth century saw an increase in union membership despite the belief of some experts that organized labor was moribund.

Before World War II, strikes were labor's most powerful tool. Although the massive and bloody confrontations of the nineteenth century are unlikely in the future, and negotiation has largely replaced work stoppages, in some places at some times the cry "Strike!" may still be heard.

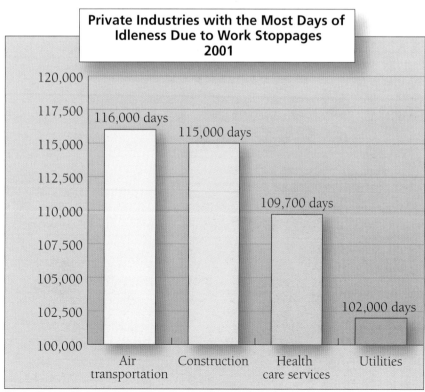

Private Industries with the Most Days of Idleness Due to Work Stoppages 2001

- Air transportation: 116,000 days
- Construction: 115,000 days
- Health care services: 109,700 days
- Utilities: 102,000 days

Source: Bureau of Labor Statistics, "Work Stoppages Summary," March 22, 2002.

Further Reading

Bimba, Anthony. *The Molly Maguires*. New York: International Publishers, 1970.

Brecher, Jeremy. *Strike!* Boston: South End Press, 1997.

Foner, Philip. *A History of the Labor Movement in the United States*. 4 vols. New York: International Publishers, 1947–1965.

Fried, Albert, ed. *Except to Walk Free: Documents and Notes in the History of American Labor*. Garden City, N.Y.: Anchor Press, 1974.

Wertheimer, Barbara. *We Were There: The Story of Working Women in America*. New York: Pantheon, 1977.

Zinn, Howard. *A People's History of the United States, 1492–Present*. New York: HarperCollins, 1999.

—*Connie Tuttle*

Subsidy

Subsidy is financial assistance granted by a government to a private person, association, or corporation to support an undertaking considered beneficial to the public. Subsidy may come in the form of direct financial contributions or it may be indirect aid, for example, tax breaks, low-interest loans, inexpensive insurance, and low purchase prices for land and natural resources. Subsidy also describes financial assistance granted by one country to another.

Every year, billions of U.S. tax dollars are spent on subsidizing a vast array of American businesses, industries, and services. In addition, the federal government regularly subsidizes other countries through, for example, liberal trade policies and direct assistance packages. The general consensus is that the United States must engage in these forms of subsidy to promote the health of the national economy and general public welfare. Rarely, however, do policy makers fully agree on who should get what. Indeed, although most agree that government subsidy of big business and industry should be reduced, enacting legislation that reflects this ideal has proven to be difficult for members of Congress, who must balance their constituents' concerns with those of the country as a whole.

Why Subsidize?

The word *subsidy* often carries a negative connotation: the media regularly warn about government spending that benefits big business and industry at the cost of American taxpayers. At the same time, U.S. subsidy policies are partly responsible for making the United States the world's leading economic power. For instance, in the nineteenth century the federal government developed a system of subsidies to encourage individuals and companies to make the high-risk move to the western states. Legislation during this time made land free for homesteaders, developed railroads, waterways, and irrigation systems, and offered rock-bottom prices for the purchase of land containing natural resources. Without these various forms of subsidy, the West would never have developed and flourished as it did. State and federal governments still apply similar subsidy principles to support the growth of new technologies in industries like defense and energy.

Subsidy has also proven to be instrumental in strengthening weakened economies. For example, in the 1930s, when the U.S. economy was ravaged by the Great Depression, Congress passed New Deal legislation, including the Agricultural Adjustment Administration, which helped to control crop overproduction by paying farmers to leave their land fallow. Other forms of subsidy, for example, the Civilian Conservation Corps and the Tennessee

See also:
Agriculture Industry; Fiscal Policy; Great Depression; International Monetary Fund; Recession.

Two U.S. Civilian Conservation Corps enrollees work on the construction of a building in Arkansas in 1937.

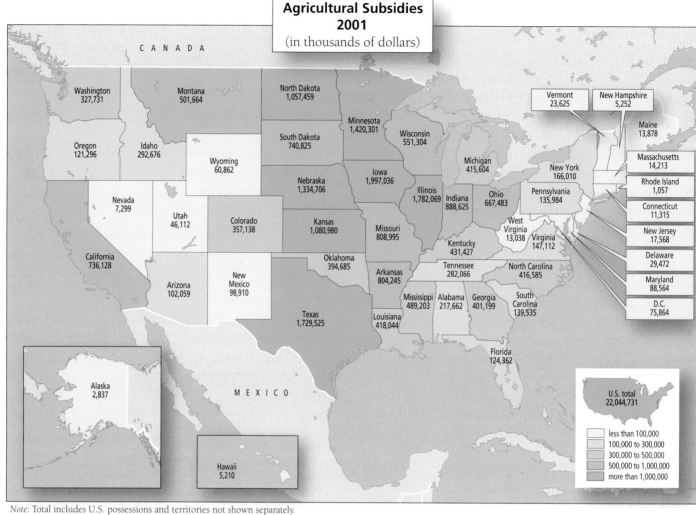

**Agricultural Subsidies
2001**

(in thousands of dollars)

CANADA

Washington
327,731

Montana
501,664

North Dakota
1,057,459

Minnesota
1,420,301

Wisconsin
551,304

Michigan
415,604

Vermont
23,625

New Hampshire
5,252

Maine
13,878

Oregon
121,296

Idaho
292,676

Wyoming
60,862

South Dakota
740,825

Iowa
1,997,036

New York
166,010

Massachusetts
14,213

Rhode Island
1,057

Nevada
7,299

Utah
46,112

Colorado
357,138

Nebraska
1,334,706

Illinois
1,782,069

Indiana
888,625

Ohio
667,483

Pennsylvania
135,984

Connecticut
11,315

New Jersey
17,568

California
736,128

Kansas
1,080,980

Missouri
808,995

Kentucky
431,427

West
Virginia
13,038

Virginia
147,112

Delaware
29,472

Maryland
88,564

Arizona
102,059

New
Mexico
98,910

Oklahoma
394,685

Arkansas
804,245

Tennessee
282,066

North Carolina
416,585

D.C.
75,864

Texas
1,729,525

Louisiana
418,044

Mississippi
489,203

Alabama
217,662

Georgia
401,199

South
Carolina
139,535

Florida
124,362

MEXICO

Alaska
2,837

Hawaii
5,210

U.S. total
22,044,731

less than 100,000
100,000 to 300,000
300,000 to 500,000
500,000 to 1,000,000
more than 1,000,000

Note: Total includes U.S. possessions and territories not shown separately.

Source: U.S. Department of Agriculture, National Agriculture Statistics Service, http://www.nass.usda.gov/research (March 23, 2003).

Valley Authority, reduced unemployment and provided environmental and development assistance to depressed regions. Although much New Deal–era legislation is no longer in effect, its principles still influence U.S. subsidy policy.

Another important form of subsidy occurs when state and federal governments help industries provide a necessary public service that would otherwise not be profitable. For example, in the 1920s the federal government began subsidizing private airlines for delivery of mail. In part because of this policy, the airline industry grew and carriers began to transport passengers. The industry is now so essential to the health of the U.S. economy that, after the 2001 terrorist attacks, Congress quickly passed a $15 billion aid package to ensure the survival of the industry.

Other industries that receive this kind of federal and state support include health care, education, railroads, and home and road construction.

With all of these tax dollars being funneled into domestic business and industry, why should the United States subsidize other countries? The United States may do so to generate goodwill, assist a war effort that is deemed important to national security, or to help stabilize a country's economy—increasingly important in an era of globalization, when one region's economic distress may effectively destabilize the world economy. The United States does not work alone in providing such subsidies. The International Monetary Fund (IMF), an organization of 183 countries, was established to encourage economic growth in member countries and promote financial cooperation. To fulfill that mission, the IMF often provides temporary financial assistance to countries that are threatened by excessive debt or currency devaluation.

Subsidy Controversies

Despite these clear benefits of subsidy, U.S. policy makers have been sharply criticized for continuing subsidy policies that primarily benefit huge corporations rather than small businesses and individuals who are more clearly in need of assistance. U.S. farm policy has come under particular scrutiny in recent years. In the first decade of the twenty-first century, $73 billion in federal subsidies will go to farms, but 47 percent of the payments go to 8 percent of the nation's farms—the wealthiest of them; 60 percent of the nation's farms receive no crop subsidies at all. Critics have demanded that the federal government reduce this level of spending and redirect it to less wealthy farms. In addition, concern has been expressed that such subsidy policies do more harm to the economy than good: because agricultural subsidies often come in the form of the government paying farmers a fixed price for crops, farmers are motivated to overproduce without regard for real market prices.

Congress has been criticized for "pork barrel" spending, or legislation that subsidizes special projects for particular districts and states. Through pork barrel spending, federal money is channeled into unnecessary military bases, prisons, and VA hospitals to keep them in operation, and waterway, bridge, and highway construction that would typically be paid for with state money. "Pork" does not benefit the country at large; it serves the narrow interests of legislators' districts and states. Thus, pork barrel spending is largely considered to be a method of securing reelection—at a cost to U.S. taxpayers of billions of dollars a year.

Such wasteful subsidy policies may go hand in hand with environmental degradation. Government-supported mining, farming, ranching, irrigation, logging, and oil

Sen. Edward Kennedy of Massachusetts meets reporters in 1997 to discuss government subsidies to businesses, sometimes called "corporate welfare."

A farmer fertilizes wheat in Tennessee, where farmers received $282 million in federal subsidies in 2001.

and gas drilling enterprises are allowed to deplete natural resources, pollute air and groundwater, and destroy whole ecosystems. Often the government foots the bill for environmental cleanup costs, rather than holding the companies themselves responsible. Taxpayer and environmental organizations like Friends of the Earth, Taxpayers for Common Sense, and U.S. PIRGs (Public Interest Research Groups) lobby Congress for reform of subsidy policies that are doubly costly in their wastefulness and the harm they do to the environment.

With special interest groups spending millions of dollars a year in lobbying on Capitol Hill, government cannot seem to wean big businesses from the federal dollar. Despite an increased show of willingness in the 1990s to cut subsidies, in practice, Congress has often done the reverse—not only maintaining but also expanding federal aid to favored industries and pork barrel projects. However, cuts in subsidy spending

must be approached with a certain amount of caution: U.S. businesses must remain competitive with other countries that provide similar subsidies to their businesses and industries. Hence, at the beginning of the twenty-first century, U.S. policy makers have a mandate to enact subsidy reforms that promote taxpayer rights at the same time that they preserve national health, economic and otherwise.

Further Reading

Chadd, Edward A. "Manifest Subsidy." *Common Cause National Magazine*, Fall 1995. http://www.ccsi.com/~comcause/news/chadd.html (March 18, 2003).

Myers, Norman, and Jennifer Kent. *Perverse Subsidies: How Misused Tax Dollars Harm the Environment and the Economy.* Washington, D.C.: Island Press, 2001.

Pye-Smith, Charlie. *The Subsidy Scandal: How Your Government Wastes Your Money to Wreck Your Environment.* Sterling, Va.: Earthscan, 2002.

—*Andrea Troyer and John Troyer*

Supply and Demand

Supply and demand are two concepts used by economists to explain how free markets work. In a free market, no central authority sets prices or decides how much of specific goods should be produced. Instead, such issues are decided by supply, demand, and the interaction between the two.

Supply and demand are abstract concepts that work perfectly only in a hypothetical universe. Nonetheless, supply and demand are useful ideas that help explain much that goes on in the real world. For example, when members of the Organization of Petroleum Exporting Countries (OPEC), an oil cartel, want to change the global price of petroleum, they agree on how much oil they will produce, confident in the knowledge that oil prices will fluctuate in a predictable fashion depending on the supply.

When economists want to pare away all the complex workings of a real-world market and boil it down to essentials, they usually end up with two types of consumers: households and business firms. The household is a unit that is basically treated as a single decision-making consumer. Each household wants to buy the goods that will make it happiest. A business firm is also a single decision-making unit, but its goal is to maximize its profits.

The Laws of Demand

Households buy goods and services, thus creating demand in a market. (The members of the household probably work and maybe rent out the basement, so they also supply certain things in the market, such as labor and living space. However, in this example, the focus is on demand.) If many households buy a lot of something, demand for that product is high. If only a few households buy a particular product, then demand is low.

How much demand a particular household creates for a particular good depends on a number of factors. One is consumer taste, or how much satisfaction or enjoyment a household will get from a good. Although trying to measure something like satisfaction might be impossible, one rule does tend to hold: the more of something people have, the less enjoyment they get from buying even more of it. Generally speaking, if a man has no shoes, he will be very motivated to buy his first pair of shoes. If he has 50 pairs of shoes, he will be less motivated to buy the fifty-first pair; instead he might spend the money on a second shirt. If a man wants a shirt and a pair of shoes equally badly and is on a tight budget, he will most likely buy whichever is cheaper to maximize the enjoyment he gets from his money.

Generally speaking, households with more money buy more, so an increase in overall income will increase demand for most goods. The exception to this rule concerns inferior goods: buyers with more money to spend tend to avoid inferior products.

The price of other items can also affect demand for a particular product. Say bagels are $2 per bag and cereal is $5 per box. If the price of cereal drops to $3 per box, fewer people will buy bagels for breakfast because cereal is so cheap—even though the price of bagels has not changed. In this case, cereal is called a substitute good, because people can substitute it for bagels.

See also:
Microeconomics; Price Controls; Pricing; Scarcity.

The price of a good has an impact on its supply: for example, if CDs can be sold for $12.99 a piece, fewer firms will be interested in producing them than if they can be sold for $17.99.

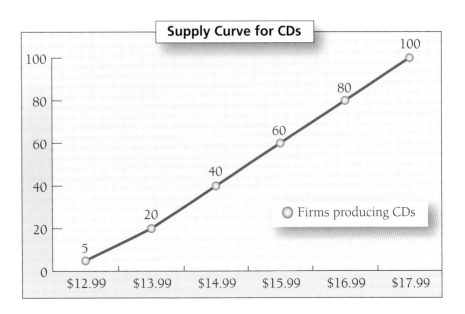

Supply Curve for CDs

○ Firms producing CDs

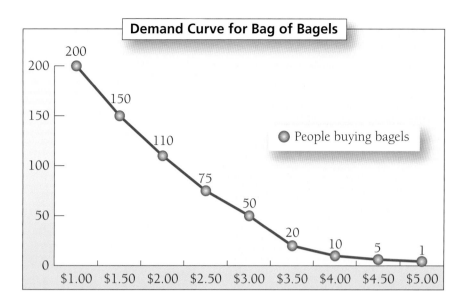

Demand Curve for Bag of Bagels

○ People buying bagels

The price of a good has an impact on its demand: if a bag of bagels costs $1.00, many people will buy it. If the same bag costs $5.00, however, far fewer people will buy it.

Bagels taste better with cream cheese, which costs $2 per tub. Assume the price of bagels holds steady, but the price of cream cheese falls to $1 per tub. Because the cream-cheese-and-bagel combination is now cheaper, more people will buy bagels, even though the price of bagels has not changed. Cream cheese is a complementary good because it is used with bagels.

Another factor influencing demand for bagels is the price of bagels. If all the other factors influencing demand stay constant—no major shifts in consumer taste, incomes unchanged, and the prices of other goods remain the same—the only thing that will affect demand for bagels is price. If bagels are costly, fewer households will buy them because they want to maximize the enjoyment they get from their money. Buying expensive bagels when cheaper cereal is available will likely seem to be a waste of money, so demand will be low. If bagels are cheap, more households will buy them and demand will be high.

A graph can be made explaining the demand for bagels; price is put on the vertical axis and the number of bagels sold on the horizontal axis. The resulting graph would slope downward from the left to right: at $5 per bag, almost no one would buy bagels; at $1 per bag, almost everyone would. This is called the law of downward sloping demand (or the law of demand): if

nothing else changes, the cheaper something is, the more it will sell.

The Laws of Supply

Supply is created by business firms—they actually own factories and make the goods that households buy. (They also buy things and therefore create demand, but for the sake of simplicity, only supply is considered here.) Firms want to make as large a profit as they can, thus they need to both generate revenues and control costs.

What determines how large a supply of something will be made? Certainly the efficiency of the manufacturing process is a factor—if a product requires vast amounts of resources and time to make, firms will make less of it. Another major factor is the cost of making the good. Making a good can entail many different costs, for example, building a factory, hiring workers, transporting the good to market.

One kind of cost that strongly affects supply is marginal cost, which is the cost of making just one more of a good—one more pair of shoes, one more bagel, one more computer chip. If a company builds a shoe factory with a capacity to make 500 pairs of shoes per day and starts out making 100 pairs of shoes, the marginal cost of making one more pair of shoes is probably fairly low—chances are the company would just have to buy some more supplies. However, if the factory is at capacity and the company is making 500 pairs of shoes each day, to make just one more pair of shoes would require that the company build a second factory—giving that 501st pair a much higher marginal cost. At that point, the company's management might decide not to make 501 pairs of shoes per day because the cost of doing so would destroy profits.

All firms can reach the point where the marginal cost is just too high. The higher a price is for a particular good, the higher that level is, and the more a company can produce while still achieving excellent profits. A graph of how much of a particular good firms would produce at a particular price would slant upward from left to right: at $25

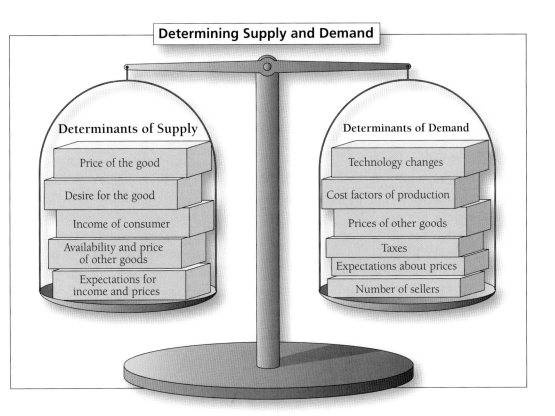

Determining Supply and Demand

Determinants of Supply

- Price of the good
- Desire for the good
- Income of consumer
- Availability and price of other goods
- Expectations for income and prices

Determinants of Demand

- Technology changes
- Cost factors of production
- Prices of other goods
- Taxes
- Expectations about prices
- Number of sellers

per pair, few firms are making shoes, but at $150 for the exact same pair, many firms make many shoes. This is the law of upward sloping supply (or law of supply). The higher the price for something, the more of it will be made.

Demand meets supply in the market. For example, imagine that many shoe firms have made many shoes, expecting to sell them for $150 per pair. (For the sake of this example, imagine the shoe market is extraordinarily simple; there is only one style and quality of shoe.) The firms offer the shoes on the market and discover that not very many people are willing to pay $150 for shoes. The result is a shoe surplus—many unsold shoes. Conversely, imagine that consumers have heard that shoes now cost $25. They flock to the market looking for $25 shoes and are sorely disappointed—the price of shoes has become so low that no firms are making them anymore and the shoe stores are empty. Such a situation is called a shortage.

In an ideal market, surpluses and shortages quickly correct themselves. Eventually one of the firms will start offering shoes at a price lower than $150, and soon the other

firms will follow suit. As the price of shoes falls, the firms start making fewer shoes and people start buying more, so the surplus is over. Likewise, if a shortage occurs, the few firms that are making shoes will start making more and charging a higher price. Other firms realize that the shoe business is worth

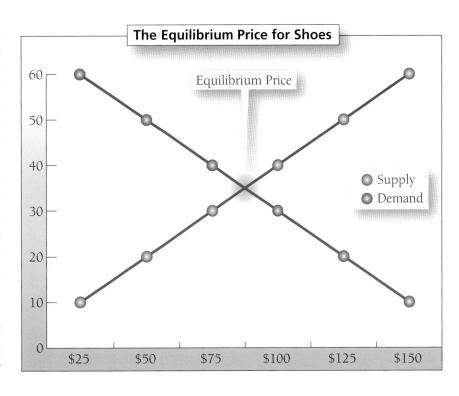

The Equilibrium Price for Shoes

Equilibrium Price

- Supply
- Demand

going into and even more shoes are made. Fewer people want to buy shoes if they cost more, and the shortage is over.

If the downward-sloping demand curve for shoes (\) is combined with the upward-sloping supply curve for shoes (/), at some point the two lines cross (X). That point is called the equilibrium price, and it represents the price where supply perfectly matches demand. At the equilibrium price of shoes, every single shoe made would be purchased, and every single household that wanted to buy shoes at that price could do so.

Obviously the equilibrium price represents an ideal that has probably never been reached in the real world. In a simplified market, the price of goods will always move toward the equilibrium price: if the price is too high, a surplus will result and it will be lowered to the equilibrium price; if the price is too low, a shortage will result and it will be raised to the equilibrium price. This tendency of prices in a market to move to the equilibrium price is known as the law of supply and demand.

Market Forces

The laws of demand, supply, and supply and demand are also sometimes called market forces, and they can wreak havoc with well-intentioned efforts to control prices. Imagine that a country is facing a shortage of wheat. Market forces come into play: the price of wheat increases, and people start using cheaper corn instead. As people in this country traditionally cook with wheat flour, not cornmeal, they are unhappy about the situation and complain to the government. The country's government declares that wheat merchants are taking

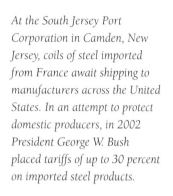

At the South Jersey Port Corporation in Camden, New Jersey, coils of steel imported from France await shipping to manufacturers across the United States. In an attempt to protect domestic producers, in 2002 President George W. Bush placed tariffs of up to 30 percent on imported steel products.

Grains and beans for sale at a market in Arles, France. If the price of one grain goes up, consumers are likely to purchase something else instead.

advantage of the shortage; the government imposes price controls on wheat, lowering the price of wheat to what it was before the shortage began.

Immediately, people stop using corn and switch back to wheat, further depleting wheat supplies. Wheat merchants do not want to sell their grain for such low prices, so they put the wheat they have into storage, expecting to sell it after the price controls are lifted. This takes even more wheat off the market. Foreign wheat merchants, who were considering entering the country's market because the price was rising, decide not to do so. Soon the moderate wheat shortage has become a serious one—wheat is officially cheap, but no one can find any to buy.

This situation has replayed itself time and time again throughout history. For example, many countries, including the United States, give subsidies and other assistance to manufacturers of steel, who have suffered as the price of steel has dropped. However, by keeping steel manufacturers in business, governments keep steel production high, so the price of steel tends not to rise and the industry never gets healthy. Supply and demand may work perfectly only in an ideal world, but they work well enough in the real world to make them worthy of attention.

Further Reading

Caplin, Andrew, and John Leahy. *Durable Goods Cycles.* Cambridge, Mass.: National Bureau of Economic Research, 1999.

Heilbroner, Robert L., and James K. Galbraith. *The Economic Problem.* 9th ed. Englewood Cliffs, N.J.: Prentice Hall, 1990.

Hirshleifer, Jack, and David Hirshleifer. *Price Theory and Applications.* Upper Saddle River, N.J.: Prentice Hall, 1998

Trescott, Paul B. *The Logic of the Price System.* New York: McGraw-Hill, 1970.

—*Mary Sisson*

Elasticity in Demand

The law of demand says that people will buy more of something if the price is lower; however, that effect is more pronounced for some goods than for others. Cell phones, for example, became widespread only after their price dropped. However, sales of the injected insulin used by people with severe diabetes would be unlikely to change much if the price rose. Those who need injected insulin to survive would still buy it even if it cost more, while those who do not need it are unlikely to buy it regardless of how cheap it is.

How sensitive demand and supply are to shifts in a good's price is called elasticity. Supply elasticity refers to how quickly companies can shift production up or down to respond to changes in price. Demand elasticity refers to how much demand shifts in response to changes in price. Price elasticity refers to how much the price will shift in response to changes in supply or demand.

For companies, the elasticity of demand for their good is a major consideration in setting prices. If demand for their good is elastic, they can sell more of it if they cut prices. If demand for their good is very, very elastic indeed—as in a highly competitive market for, say, cell phones—they can quickly dominate a market by undercutting their competition just a little bit. If demand for their good is inelastic, then cutting prices will not result in more sales and will only lower revenues.

Sustainable Development

Historically, environmental protection has been considered the enemy of economic growth. Sustainable development strives to reconcile these two goals, meeting the needs of the present without compromising the ability of future generations to meet their own needs. The concept has revolutionized the way in which many businesses view environmental issues. Nevertheless, the concept is problematic and controversial, and its usefulness for solving Earth's ongoing environmental crisis remains uncertain.

What Is Sustainable Development?

Until recently, economists and environmentalists seldom saw eye-to-eye. The publication of *The Limits to Growth* (1972), an influential but highly pessimistic report by

A crowded train station in Bhopal, India, in 1984; more than 200,000 people were forced to flee the city because of the Union Carbide industrial accident that killed 2,500 people and injured another 50,000.

the Club of Rome, a think tank concerned with global problems, prompted a debate on whether unchecked economic growth threatened to severely deplete natural resources. In *Small Is Beautiful* (1973), British environmentalist E. F. Schumacher advocated lower economic growth and small-scale local development to protect the environment. Oxford economist Wilfred Beckerman replied with an argument that "small is stupid" because "economic growth is still a necessary condition for remedying most of the serious environmental problems facing the world, particularly in developing countries."

The concept of sustainable development suggested a way of moving beyond this polarized economy-versus-environment debate. The basic concept of sustainable development is the belief that economic development can proceed without exhausting the natural resources on which all life ultimately depends.

If environmentalists view sustainable development as a way to control what they

consider to be the worst excesses of industry and commerce, businesses see the concept as a new path to competitive advantage. According to H. N. J. Smits, CEO and chairman of Dutch banking group Radobank, "Sustainable development, far from being a new and restrictive condition to industrial and financial progress, provides the keys that will unlock all the major markets of the future." For example, oil companies might redefine themselves as energy supply companies and base their businesses on sustainable energy forms like solar power. This would bring not just environmental benefits but also ensure the longer-term viability and profitability of oil companies as petroleum reserves dwindle.

Political entities like the European Union also note the economic advantages of sustainable development; Europe's 15 member states adopted their first joint sustainability strategy in June 2001, arguing that the strategy would deal "with economic, social and environmental policies in a mutually reinforcing way." The World Business Council on Sustainable Development confirms this view: "Sustainable development is about ensuring a better quality of life for everyone, now and for generations to come. Thus it combines ecological, social, and economic concerns, and offers business opportunities for companies that can improve the lives of the world's people."

Several attempts have been made to define sustainable development more clearly. A 1987 report, *Our Common Future* (also known as the Brundtland report after its chair, Norwegian politician Gro Harlem Brundtland), proposed that key elements of sustainable development include: using growth to eliminate poverty and meet basic human needs in developing countries; conserving and enhancing natural resources; developing environmentally appropriate technologies; and combining economic and environmental factors in decision-making processes. Others have since offered strategies for realizing the promise of sustainable development. In 1991 the International Chamber of Commerce published a 16-point

Business Charter for Sustainable Development, which seeks to integrate environmental concerns into key aspects of business management, including customer relations, employee training, and relationships with vendors and suppliers.

For all these attempts at clarification, no single definition of sustainable development has emerged. Indeed, as *Economist* environment editor Frances Cairncross has written: "The appeal of the phrase is that it means so many different things to different people. Every environmentally aware politician is in favor of it, a sure sign that they do not know what it means."

The Pros and Cons of Sustainable Development

The value of the sustainable development concept may depend less on how clearly it can be defined than on how much of a difference it makes in practice. Supporters of the idea point to considerable progress in some industries, but critics remain doubtful. Forestry, for example, has witnessed high-profile initiatives like the Forestry Stewardship Council (FSC), an international labeling initiative that encourages consumers to choose wood products harvested from sustainable forests and to avoid timber from tropical rain forests. However, according to the FSC, only about 0.02 percent of the world's forests are managed sustainably. Moreover, economic studies suggest that, although global incentives to conserve

> Humanity has the ability to make development sustainable—to ensure that it meets the needs of the present without compromising the ability of future generations to meet their own needs. The concept of sustainable development does imply limits— not absolute limits but limitations imposed by the present state of technology and social organization on environmental resources and by the ability of the biosphere to absorb the effects of human activities. But technology and social organization can be both managed and improved to make way for a new era of economic growth. The commission believes that widespread poverty is no longer inevitable. Poverty is not only an evil in itself, but sustainable development requires meeting the basic needs of all and extending to all the opportunity to fulfill their aspirations for a better life. A world in which poverty is endemic will always be prone to ecological and other catastrophes.
>
> —*Our Common Future* (The Brundtland Report), World Commission on Environment and Development, 1987

U.N. Commission on Sustainable Development Indicators

Social	Environmental	Economic	Institutional
Equity • Poverty • Gender equality **Health** • Nutritional status • Mortality • Sanitation • Drinking water • Health care delivery **Education** • Education level • Literacy **Living conditions** • Housing • Security (crime) • Population (population change)	**Atmosphere** • Climate change • Ozone layer depletion • Air quality **Land** • Agriculture • Forests • Desertification • Urbanization **Oceans, seas, and coasts** • Coastal zone • Fisheries **Fresh water** • Water quantity • Water quality **Biodiversity** • Ecosystem • Species	**Economic structure** • Economic performance • Trade • Financial status **Consumption and production patterns** • Material consumption • Energy use • Waste generation and management • Transportation	**Institutional framework** • Strategic implementation of sustainable development strategy • International cooperation **Institutional capacity** • Information access • Science and technology • Disaster preparedness and response

The U.N. Commission on Sustainable Development has outlined a large number of indicators, which include social, economic, institutional, and environmental factors.

Source: U.N. Commission on Sustainable Development, "Indicators of Sustainable Development," http://www.un.org/esa/sustdev (March 10, 2003).

forests or manage them sustainably may be in place, old-style industrial logging continues to provide much better financial returns, especially from a national perspective—a major disincentive to the adoption of sustainable development practices.

Other industries have also moved toward sustainability. The chemical industry in North America, Europe, and Australia has established a program called Responsible Care that, among other achievements, has encouraged companies to reduce toxic emissions, communicate with local communities, and persuade suppliers to join them on a journey of progressive environmental improvement. Critics argue that voluntary regulatory programs are simply a ruse to avoid tougher, government-imposed regulations in the aftermath of chemical disasters like the explosion at the Union Carbide chemical factory in Bhopal, India, in 1984.

Sustainable development is problematic for other reasons. One difficulty is that some industries can more easily integrate the concept into their operations. Information technology companies find sustainable development much easier to embrace than, for example, oil companies, whose core business, according to most definitions, can never be remotely sustainable.

Another problem is the difficulty of assessing whether local efforts toward sustainable development are having a similar effect on a global scale. For example, cities

Achieving Sustainable Development

In its April 2001 report *Sustainability through the Market*, the World Business Council on Sustainable Development suggested seven keys to sustainability:

• increasing innovation (developing "new ways to improve lives while boosting business");
• practicing eco-efficiency (for example, implementing energy-saving technologies that save more money than they cost);
• increasing dialogue between companies, governments, and local communities;
• influencing customer choices by making the benefits of sustainability clearer and more compelling;
• encouraging markets to take more account of environmental and social concerns;
• using markets to reach and improve the lives of the poorest people;
• and "establishing the worth of Earth"—making sure the true environmental and social costs of our use of resources are appreciated.

in industrialized nations have achieved major improvements in air and water quality over recent decades through tougher legislation and greater public awareness of environmental issues. Some of these gains are the result of the gradual transition from manufacturing to service economies in the developed world. Yet developed countries still need manufactured goods, many of which are now produced in developing countries that have less stringent environmental regulations. Sustainability gains in developed nations may, therefore, have been counterbalanced by environmental and social losses in developing nations.

Some environmentalists view the concept of sustainable development with suspicion, believing it may be used as a public relations exercise to disguise business-as-usual industrial attitudes with environmental platitudes—a technique these environmentalists call "greenwash." They cite, for example, the way oil companies have set up token solar energy ventures, while simultaneously supporting organizations like the Global Climate Coalition, a Washington, D.C.–based lobby that campaigns against the science of climate change and the political efforts to address it. Economists like Wilfred Beckerman are also skeptical: "If 'sustainable development' is interpreted . . . as implying that all other components of welfare are to be sacrificed in the interests of preserving the environment in the form it happens to be in today, then it is morally indefensible."

Overall, so-called sustainability indicators, for example, plummeting fish stocks, animal species in decline, rising human population in developing nations, and deteriorating freshwater resources, suggest the world has never been further from sustainable development. According to Dr. James Baker, head of the U.S. National Oceanic and Atmospheric Administration, "there is a global consensus that we must make our development sustainable." That much is evident in statements from organizations, the World Bank, for instance, which argue for sustainable economic

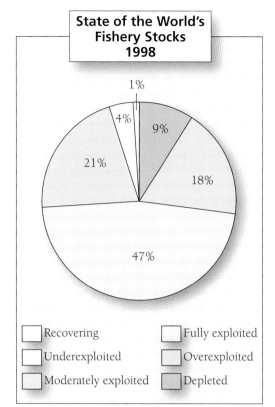

State of the World's Fishery Stocks 1998

1%
4%
9%
18%
21%
47%

☐ Recovering   ☐ Fully exploited
☐ Underexploited   ☐ Overexploited
☐ Moderately exploited   ☐ Depleted

Source: United Nations Food and Agriculture Organization, *World Agriculture: Towards 2015/30*, 2002.

One indicator of the degree to which sustainable development has or has not been achieved is world fish stocks, many of which are overexploited.

growth that can eradicate poverty, and the World Business Council on Sustainable Development, which highlights the profitable business opportunities offered by improving people's lives.

Further Reading

Beckerman, Wilfred. *Small Is Stupid: Blowing the Whistle on the Greens.* London: Duckworth, 1995.

Cairncross, Frances. *Green Inc.: A Guide to Business and the Environment.* Washington, D.C.: Island Press, 1995.

Holliday, Chad, Stephan Schmidheiny, and Philip Watts. *Walking the Talk: The Business Case for Sustainable Development.* San Francisco: Berrett-Koehler Publishers, 2002.

Kirkby, John, Phil O'Keefe, and Lloyd Timberlake, eds. *The Earthscan Reader in Sustainable Development.* London: Earthscan, 1995.

Myers, Norman. "Sustainable Consumption." *Science* 287 (March 31, 2000): 2419.

Reinhardt, Forest. "Bringing the Environment Down to Earth." *Harvard Business Review* (July-August 1999): 149.

World Commission on Environment and Development. *Our Common Future.* Oxford: Oxford University Press, 1987.

—*Chris Woodford*

Taft–Hartley Act

In 1935 the National Labor Relations Act (NLRA; also called the Wagner Act) was passed by Congress to regulate interstate commerce and govern the management–union relationship on a national level. When the NLRA was passed, pro-union sentiment in the United States was quite strong. Twelve years later, a number of factors converged to create a groundswell of antiunion sentiment, including a series of large-scale strikes, management fears of the increasing power of unions, and widespread suspicions of fraud and communist infiltration of unions. Sponsored by Sen. Robert Taft of Ohio and Rep. Fred A. Hartley of New Jersey, the Labor Management Relations Act of 1947 (usually referred to as the Taft–Hartley Act) amended the NLRA, aiming to address these perceived abuses of power by unions.

Taft–Hartley expanded the power of the National Labor Relations Board to hear disputes between employees and employers, and it granted employees the right to collectively bargain under union auspices. However, Taft–Hartley also weakened labor unions significantly, in particular by setting strict limits on engaging in strikes, and by giving employees the right not to join a labor union or choose not to participate in collective bargaining.

Taft–Hartley established control of labor disputes by prohibiting wildcat (unannounced) strikes; the legislation requires that unions serve advance notice of an impending strike and pursue government mediation before ending a collective bargaining agreement. Under the Taft–Hartley revision of the NLRA, the federal government was given the power to forbid strikes—defined as either the halt, "slowing down," or interruption of work initiated by employees—when the strike jeopardizes national health or safety. Employers were given the right to file a lawsuit to recover damages if the strike can be deemed to be unlawful under the legislation. Taft–Hartley also specifies that government employees who strike will lose employment; President Ronald Reagan used this legislation to fire striking air traffic controllers in 1981.

Concerns about the increasing political activism of unions prompted the framers of Taft–Hartley to place political restraints on labor union organizers and restricted unions from making contributions to federal campaigns or elections. The ban on political contributions by unions was removed after a series of lawsuits in federal court. Taft–Hartley also weakened labor unions by giving more

A cartoon from the New York Mirror *in 1952 shows President Harry Truman refusing to be rescued by a Taft–Hartley life preserver. The cartoon refers to Truman's unwillingness to invoke Taft–Hartley to postpone a steel strike.*

rights to employers and excluding certain industries from having to comply with National Labor Relations Board regulations.

Taft–Hartley did offer a few new protections for employees, including Section 143, called the Saving Provisions, which is a precautionary antislavery clause. Section 143 ensures that employees may not be forced into labor without their consent and allows employees to quit work. Section 143 states that nothing in the act "shall be construed to require an individual employee to render labor or service without his consent" nor "construed to make the quitting of labor by an employee an illegal act." Irrespective of Taft–Hartley's protections for employees, it is generally viewed as pro-business legislation. Penalties for noncompliance with Taft–Hartley range from loss of employment to incarceration.

U.S. labor policy was further amended by the Landrum–Griffin Act of 1959, which focuses on improper labor and management activities, violence by labor union leaders, and "diversion and misuse of labor union funds by high-ranking officials." The 1959 act regulates internal union activities and issues, including funding. Communists are required to leave the Communist Party and wait five years before holding a union office. The amendments also prohibit direct targeting of business partners of companies subject to union action (i.e., secondary boycotting) and picketing corporations that recognize a rival union.

Further Reading

Legal Information Institute. "Law about Labor." http://www.law.cornell.edu/topics/labor.html (March 18, 2003).

Lichtenstein, Nelson. *State of the Union: A Century of American Labor*. Princeton, N.J.: Princeton University Press, 2002.

Nelson, Daniel. *Shifting Fortunes: The Rise and Decline of American Labor, from the 1820s to the Present*. Chicago: Ivan R. Dee, 1997.

—Walter C. Farrell, Jr., Douglas Bynum, and Renee Sartin Kirby

Open and Closed Shops

Open shop and *closed shop* are terms used to designate whether all the employees in a company or factory belong to a union. A closed shop is one in which all employees are required to join a union before they can be hired by the company. An open shop is one in which employees are not required to join the union but may do so if they wish.

Unions of the late nineteenth and early twentieth centuries almost unanimously preferred the closed-shop system. In a closed shop, the unions have a great deal more power in negotiations with management because, if workers' demands are not met, the union can take the factory's entire labor force out on strike. Proponents of the closed shop argue that as every employee benefits from the advantages gained by the union, requiring every employee to pay union dues is not unreasonable.

Proponents of open shops, on the other hand, believe compelling every employee to pay union dues is coercive and unfair. They also argue that because unions have so much power in a closed-shop system, employers often cannot run their businesses efficiently; for instance, employment is not "at will" and firing incompetent employees can be difficult. Closed shops were made illegal by the Taft–Hartley Act.

A compromise between a closed shop and an open shop is a union shop, in which an employee need not be a member of the union to be hired but is expected to join the union after an initial training period. Many states have outlawed union shops, but as yet no federal statute prohibits them.

—Colleen Sullivan

Tariff

A tariff is a tax associated with the import or export of goods and services. These taxes are also referred to as customs duties. Tariffs can be structured as a percentage of the price of the item or as a flat, per unit tax. For instance, the government could place a tariff of 10 percent on all imported automobiles; this charge is referred to as an ad valorem tariff (*ad valorem* is Latin for "according to the value"). Alternatively, the government could simply charge a flat rate of $1,500 per automobile; such charge is called a specific tariff.

Tariffs have a long history and have been used quite extensively throughout U.S. history as a way for the federal government to raise tax revenues. Prior to the creation of the federal income tax in 1913, a major portion of U.S. government revenues came from tariffs on trade. In 1900 tariff revenues contributed about 50 percent to federal government revenues. Later in the century, however, tariff revenues had shrunk dramatically to only about 1.5 percent of federal government revenues.

Between 1945 and 2001 the worldwide level of tariffs was reduced by almost 95 percent as a result of two factors. First, the General Agreement on Tariffs and Trade (GATT) specifically targeted tariffs for reduction within a multilateral, mutually negotiated framework. Second, as tariffs have fallen out of favor, a pernicious cousin to the tariff—quotas—has risen to take their place as the preferred method of protecting domestic industries and their workers.

Tariffs violate economic efficiency because they reduce the gains from trades that accrue through specialization and exchange. The logic of gains from trade extends from trade among individuals to trade among complex societies. The initial reason for people to trade is either to obtain something they do not have access to or to take advantage of the productivity gains inherent to specialization and exchange. When one party specializes in the production of, say, automobiles, many productivity gains result. However, for specialization to be worthwhile, people must be free to trade. To the extent that tariffs reduce trade, they reduce productivity gains.

Because tariffs create both winners and losers in the economic system, they are linked to the concept of protectionism. The following example uses the United States and a $50 tariff on imported bicycles to illustrate the effects of a tariff. At least six important groups are affected when tariffs are placed on bicycles: foreign bicycle producers, foreign bicycle workers, domestic bicycle producers, domestic bicycle workers, domestic bicycle consumers, and the government.

Under the tariff, foreign bicycle producers are required to pay $50 for each bicycle exported to the United States; they would treat the charge as a cost of production. As a direct result, the price of imported foreign bicycles rises. Domestic consumers respond by buying fewer foreign bicycles. Therefore, foreign producers and their workers lose

A cartoon from 1921 mocks the Republican Party's reliance on tariffs.

CURES ALL THE ILLS OF MAN OR BEAST

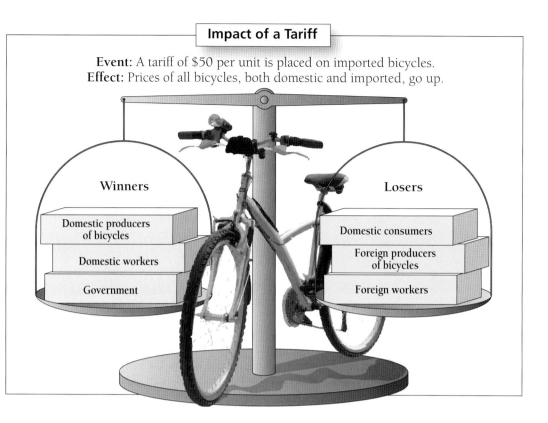

Impact of a Tariff

Event: A tariff of $50 per unit is placed on imported bicycles.
Effect: Prices of all bicycles, both domestic and imported, go up.

Winners

Domestic producers
of bicycles

Domestic workers

Government

Losers

Domestic consumers

Foreign producers
of bicycles

Foreign workers

under the tariff. On the other hand, a tariff will benefit domestic bicycle producers and workers. As the prices of the imported bicycles rise, consumers will buy more domestic bicycles because their price, relative to foreign bicycles, has fallen.

The fifth group affected is domestic consumers of bicycles. Consumer choice becomes increasingly limited, and the tariff is a tax that ultimately increases the price of all bicycles—both imported and domestic. The final major group affected by a tariff is the government, which receives the tariff revenues of $50 per bicycle. States are banned from imposing tariffs so, in the United States, the federal government receives all tariff revenues. Thus, the winners under a tariff are domestic producers and workers in the import-competing industry and the government. The losers are domestic consumers, foreign producers, and foreign workers.

The pattern of winners and losers creates a tendency for government to enact tariffs: domestic industries and organized labor are typically well represented in lobbying the government for favorable treatment. This effort is aided by two realities faced by consumers. First, most consumers know little about how

tariffs affect prices. Second, consumers, unlike industries, are not a well-organized group with lobbying power capable of delivering votes and making campaign contributions.

Further Reading

Coughlin, Cletis C., K. Alex Chrystal, and Geoffrey E. Wood. "Protectionist Trade Policies: A Survey of Theory, Evidence and Rationale." *Federal Reserve Bank of Saint Louis Review* (January–February 1988): 12-29.

Roberts, Russell. *The Choice: A Fable of Free Trade and Protectionism.* Rev. ed. Paramus, N.J.: Prentice Hall PTR, 2000.

—*Bradley K. Hobbs*

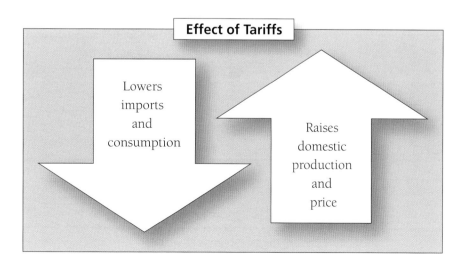

Effect of Tariffs

Lowers imports and consumption

Raises domestic production and price

See also:
Capital; Cash Flow; Income
Distribution; Internal
Revenue Service; Savings
and Investment Options.

Taxation

Taxation is the generation of revenue from fees imposed on the purchase of goods, services, property, and membership (in the case of a tax on persons, such as a head tax). A country's tax system is the primary means by which governments extract revenues from the economy needed to pay for the government and its programs. Taxation has a considerable effect on business decisions, which affect the overall health of an economy. Economists generally characterize a tax system by how well it addresses four objectives: fairness, simplicity, efficiency, and sufficiency of revenue generation.

Fairness is normally measured by ability to pay, distribution of income, and beneficiary of service (or good). Ability to pay implies that taxpayers should not be taxed to the point where they will be unable to support themselves. Distribution of income deals with the effect that taxes have on different income groups. A progressive tax, such as the U.S. income tax, places a greater burden on people with higher incomes; a progressive tax will ideally redistribute income from the wealthier sections of the economy to the poorer. Sales taxes are sometimes described as regressive because the same tax burden is placed on everyone who purchases the good, regardless of the economic condition of the purchaser. The concept of beneficiary of service (or good) calls for taxpayers to pay directly for a

Objectives of the U.S. Tax System

- Fairness
- Simplicity
- Efficiency
- Sufficiency of revenue generation

service that they use. A toll charge on a road is an example: only people who use (benefit from) the road are subjected to the toll.

Simplicity in a tax considers the degree to which a tax is computable by both taxpayers and tax collection authorities. Ideally, the amount of tax owed should be easily known. Businesses in the United States spend vast sums of money each year to determine their income tax obligations. Simplifying the nation's income tax system would reduce the complexity and number of forms required to file tax returns. Thus, simplicity ultimately reduces the compliance cost of the tax.

Efficiency looks at how tax-influenced decisions affect the economy. Every business is concerned with making regular and sustainable profits. For a tax to be efficient, its existence should not persuade a business to invest in office buildings when it might have more usefully invested in a factory. From the perspective of a particular businessperson, the well-being of her business takes precedence over the well-being of the overall economy. For example, if a corporation decides to close a production plant because of the expense of a corporate income tax (a tax imposed on corporations' profits), the average amount that the plant would have earned is considered a loss to the economy. The decision to close the plant may be bad for the economy, but from the individual company's perspective, the decision is sound because operating with the corporate income tax would not be profitable.

In addition to the question of economic efficiency, the previous example also raises the issue of incentives. Economists study how a tax system induces individuals and firms to purchase or not purchase capital (human-made goods used to produce other goods and services) by offering various tax-saving

Effect of Insufficient Tax Revenue

Tax system produces insufficient revenue.

⬇

Government borrows funds, competing with business.

⬇

Added demand for funds raises interest rates.

⬇

Higher interest rates reduce capital investment.

⬇

Future growth potential lowered.

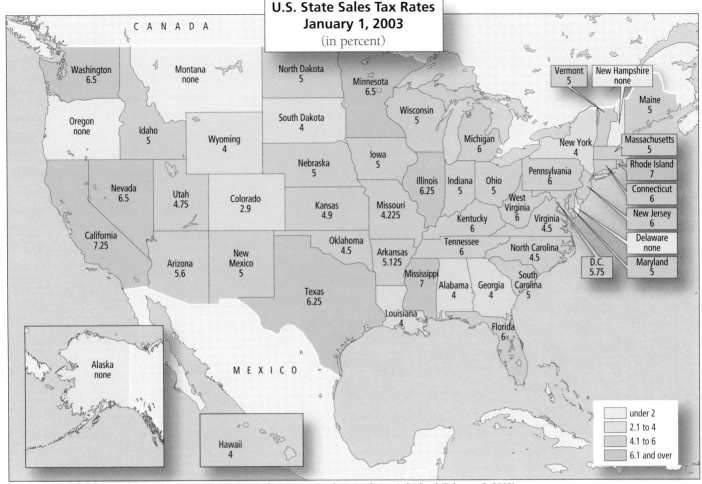

U.S. State Sales Tax Rates
January 1, 2003
(in percent)

Washington 6.5
Montana none
North Dakota 5
Minnesota 6.5
Vermont 5
New Hampshire none
Maine 5
Oregon none
Idaho 5
Wyoming 4
South Dakota 4
Wisconsin 5
Michigan 6
New York 4
Massachusetts 5
Rhode Island 7
Nevada 6.5
Utah 4.75
Colorado 2.9
Nebraska 5
Iowa 5
Illinois 6.25
Indiana 5
Ohio 5
Pennsylvania 6
Connecticut 6
New Jersey 6
California 7.25
Kansas 4.9
Missouri 4.225
Kentucky 6
West Virginia 6
Virginia 4.5
Delaware none
Maryland 5
Arizona 5.6
New Mexico 5
Oklahoma 4.5
Arkansas 5.125
Tennessee 6
North Carolina 4.5
D.C. 5.75
Texas 6.25
Mississippi 7
Alabama 4
Georgia 4
South Carolina 5
Louisiana 4
Florida 6
Alaska none
Hawaii 4

CANADA
MEXICO

under 2
2.1 to 4
4.1 to 6
6.1 and over

Source: Federation of Tax Administrators, "State Sales Tax Rates," http://www.taxadmin.org/fta/rate/sales.html (February 3, 2003).

incentives (deductions, exceptions, and so on). Economic distortions are created when firms are persuaded by tax considerations to hoard cash surpluses or enter into dubious mergers and acquisitions rather than pay greater dividends to stockholders.

Even sales taxes enter into pricing decisions. A sales tax is imposed on the consumer at the point of sale. The seller receives the price paid by the consumer minus the sales tax (which is paid to the government). Production decisions are made based on this lower price. Thus, buying decisions are made at one price and production decisions at another price, which results in an inefficiency to the economy at large.

The final characteristic to consider about tax systems is whether the system generates sufficient funds for the government. A tax system that does not generate enough revenue will cause the government to borrow funds. Government borrowing affects business by competing for limited funds in the financial markets. The added demand by the government for funds results in higher interest rates on capital investments (assuming all else remains the same). Higher interest rates cause business to reduce capital investments and thus reduce future growth potential.

Taxation is an important consideration in the making of business decisions. A tax imposed by the government offers possible gains and losses to a business; management must incorporate the tax code into the bottom line. The government must consider the impact of taxation on business decisions in the designing of the tax system.

Further Reading

Slemrod, Joel, and Jon Bakija. *Taxing Ourselves: A Citizen's Guide to the Great Debate over Tax Reform.* Cambridge, Mass.: MIT Press, 2001.

Tucker, Irvin B. *Microeconomics for Today.* Mason, Ohio: South-Western Thomson Learning, 2002.

—*James K. Self*

See also:

AFL-CIO; Labor Union; Landrum–Griffin Act; National Labor Relations Act; New Deal; Strikes.

Teamsters Union

Teamsters date to the earliest days of the United States. From colonial times onward, they were the men who drove horse-drawn wagons from the East to the expanding western frontier, contributing greatly to the economy of the young republic. A teamster's life was difficult and poverty not uncommon. By 1898 teamsters had formed into 18 local unions. In 1903, at the urging of Samuel Gompers, a leader of the American Federation of Labor, the Team Drivers International Union and the Teamsters National Union joined to form the International Brotherhood of Teamsters, Chauffeurs, Warehousemen and Helpers of America (usually referred to as the Teamsters).

In the early years of the union, Teamsters presence was strong in Chicago, New York, Boston, and St. Louis. Chicago's membership alone constituted approximately half the total union membership. In 1905 an unsuccessful strike against Montgomery Ward, a department store in Chicago, resulted in a temporary decline in membership. Daniel J. Tobin became Teamsters president in 1907, holding the position until 1952. Under his direction, the union continued to grow; by 1940 the Teamsters was the largest union in the country, and remains the largest to this day.

Changes in technology brought changes to the union. The year 1912 marked the first transcontinental delivery of goods by motorized truck. Recognizing what this meant to the union's future, Tobin began to organize long-distance truckers. The process proved bloody and violent. Eventually the Teamsters won contracts, shorter work weeks, and the right to overtime compensation for its members.

During World War I, the Teamsters participated in the war effort by moving troops and supplies from ports to battle lines in Europe. The industrial boom in the United States following the war helped the Teamsters in its organizing efforts, and by 1925 the union's treasury had amassed $1 million.

The stock market crash in 1929 ushered in over a decade of poverty and despair for Americans. By 1933 Teamsters membership had dropped to 75,000. Two years later intense organizing efforts had brought its membership to 146,000. During these difficult years, the Teamsters found an ally in President Franklin D. Roosevelt. The National Labor Relations Act, a milestone for collective bargaining (the right to have a union representative negotiate on behalf of the entire union membership), passed during Roosevelt's administration. The act codified

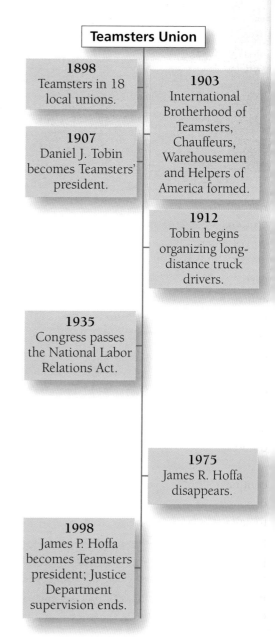

Teamsters Union

1898
Teamsters in 18 local unions.

1903
International Brotherhood of Teamsters, Chauffeurs, Warehousemen and Helpers of America formed.

1907
Daniel J. Tobin becomes Teamsters' president.

1912
Tobin begins organizing long-distance truck drivers.

1935
Congress passes the National Labor Relations Act.

1975
James R. Hoffa disappears.

1998
James P. Hoffa becomes Teamsters president; Justice Department supervision ends.

Teamsters president James R. Hoffa, right, talks with Robert F. Kennedy, chief counsel for the U.S. Senate's investigation into improper activities in labor and management, 1958.

workers' rights to collective bargaining and protected unions from management obstruction of union activity.

World War II saw the Teamsters again participating in the war effort both abroad and at home, ferrying troops and supplies from ports to battle lines. At home, Teamsters promoted the sale of war bonds and organized efforts for the collection of scrap metal and rubber, products useful in the manufacture of military supplies. Tobin took an active part in urging other labor leaders to suspend labor struggles for the duration of the war.

After the war, Teamsters membership continued to grow; by 1949 it stood at over one million. The union's tactic of threatening to halt deliveries to uncooperative employers proved extremely effective. The Teamsters' postwar expansion of its membership base to include the automotive trade, food processing, dairy, and vending machine industries contributed to its rising numbers.

At the union's 1952 convention, Tobin retired after 45 years of leadership and Dave Beck was named his successor. The 1950s were difficult for the Teamsters. Charges of corruption plagued the union, and both Beck and his successor, James R. Hoffa, were sentenced to federal prison. Testimony provided by Beck and Hoffa during Senate investigative hearings helped spur passage of the 1959 Landrum–Griffin Act; in addition to other provisions, the act provided for regulation of union affairs and control of union funds.

The 1970s and 1980s brought more difficulties. A number of Teamsters leaders were convicted of mismanagement of union funds and of taking bribes from employers. After being released from prison in 1971, James R. Hoffa disappeared in 1975. Some believe he was murdered by members of organized crime. In 1981 union president Roy Williams was convicted of bribing a United States senator, and in 1985 another

Teamsters president James P. Hoffa (son of James R. Hoffa) leads drivers in a march in Washington, D.C., in March 2000.

union president, Jackie Presser, was indicted for embezzling union funds and giving criminals unofficial jobs. In 1989 Teamsters president William McCarthy was involved in a federal racketeering suit that accused union officials of allowing crime figures to exploit the union.

Under supervision of a court-appointed trustee, the 1991 election saw reform candidate Ronald R. Carey win the union's presidency. In 1998 James P. Hoffa, the son of James R. Hoffa, replaced Carey. With Hoffa at the helm, the Teamsters came to the end of 10 years of supervision by the Justice Department. Following a successful strike against UPS in 1997, the Teamsters remained a strong presence in the labor–management arena, entering the new century with 1.5 million members and a revised code of ethics.

Further Reading

Brill, Steven. *The Teamsters*. New York: Pocket Books, 1979.

Romer, Sam. *The International Brotherhood of Teamsters: Its Government and Structure*. New York: John Wiley & Sons, 1962.

—Connie Tuttle

Technology

Advances in technology are a key element of the economic machine that generates wealth. Wealth is not only money, but also a combination of money, assets, and investments. A wealthy person can have relatively little cash but be a millionaire based on investments and assets. In the Information Age, knowledge generates wealth—knowledge products, knowledge that builds on technology, and the willingness to share knowledge with others.

This kind of wealth generator is relatively new, beginning at the end of the twentieth century with the advent of computers, the World Wide Web, and satellite communications. Previously, machines had generated wealth, and before machines, land was the generator and measure of wealth. Each shift in wealth generation relates to specific changes in technology. These shifts influenced everything from commerce to education to community structure.

The Agrarian Age (until 1760)

Hand tools ushered in the Agrarian Age, but the single most important technological advance was the plow. This simple machine allowed people to settle on the land and mass-produce food for sale in the local market. Land ownership, usually in the form of a family farm, was the primary means of generating wealth. Two classes of people—those who owned land and those who did not—arose.

The economy was fairly simple and needs-driven. Exchange of goods was a one-to-one transaction. Market area was limited by transportation—a horse and cart. Farmers either brought produce to the local market to sell or exchanged their produce for other goods. Cash might be used to purchase household goods or to reinvest in the farming operation. Reinvestment might include seed, tools, or more land.

The business organization was also simple. Farming was a family operation, and the business structure followed the structure of the extended family. The Agrarian Age overall was defined by self-sufficiency. As the economy was based on human labor, the most valued asset was a diligent, hard worker.

Changes in the textile industry in England in the latter part of the Agrarian Age helped usher in the Industrial Age. As demand for cotton cloth increased, inventors focused their attention on increasing output. The flying shuttle weaving loom (1733) and the spinning jenny (1764), a mechanical spinning wheel, were the first in a series of inventions that would eventually move the textile industry from a rural cottage industry to factories in the cities.

The Industrial Age (1760 to 1960)

The Industrial Age began in England with the use of machines to multiply the output of individual workers. The Industrial Revolution was powered first by water, then by steam, then by electricity. Textile and grain mills operated along rivers initially, using power generated by water wheels. The invention of the steam engine not only freed the factory from the river, it also changed both transportation and the power to produce goods. Steam power multiplied the "man power" of each worker by approximately 100. As the demand for goods increased, the distribution network grew. Railroads could carry goods farther and faster than the previous modes of horsepower and canals. England became the world's first industrial powerhouse.

The United States did not enter the Industrial Age until much later. In 1776

See also:
E-Business; Information Technology; Internet; Just-in-Time Inventory.

	Economy	Means of generating wealth	Exchange of goods
Agrarian Age (to 1760)	Simple; needs-driven	Land	One-to-one
Industrial Age (1760 to 1960)	Supply-driven	Factories and machinery; ownership of raw materials	One-to-many
Information Age (1960–)	Demand-driven	Knowledge	Many-to-many

Technology and the Economy

The Luddites

Advances in technology are often hailed as progress, but that opinion is not universal. Throughout history many have resisted the social changes wrought by technical innovations. In early nineteenth century England, the Luddites, a secret society of embittered textile workers, rose to fame by destroying the factory machines that were threatening their livelihood.

In 1811 mill owners began receiving letters from "General Ned Ludd" and his "Army of Redressers," threatening to destroy textile machines. One of these machines could do in a day what a skilled textile worker took a week to accomplish, and the new technology was quickly ruining an entire way of life. The workers' anger and desperation was exacerbated by an already poor economic climate: England was facing one of the worst eras of trade depression in more than 50 years.

Most Luddite attacks were very similar. A well-organized group, complete with armed sentries, entered a mill and destroyed the machines, often in full view of the mill owners. In their first year of activity, the Luddites smashed an estimated 1,000 machines, at a cost of £6,000 to £10,000.

In April 1812, near the height of Luddite violence, armed guards thwarted the Luddites' efforts at Rawford Mills. In the end, two workers were mortally wounded. One week later, Luddites murdered an anti-Luddite mill owner, William Horsfall. By then, frame breaking had been made a serious crime, and 64 Luddites were indicted. In January 1813 they were brought to trial: 24 were found guilty, 17 were hanged. The executions stopped the Luddite movement. In June 1816, during another trade slump, violence briefly resurfaced when Luddites attacked two mills in Longborough, smashing 53 frames. By the 1820s, though, Luddism had died off.

In the contemporary world, violent attacks against modern machines like computers are quite rare. However, the spirit of the movement, which is based in the preservation of prevailing culture in the face of technology, remains alive. Contemporary "neo-Luddites" rail against the society-destroying effects of technology and globalization, much as the Luddites railed against industrialization.

—*Laura Lambert*

An undated illustration depicts the destruction of a spinning jenny in Industrial Revolution–era England.

around 90 percent of the people in the United States still lived on farms. The invention of the cotton gin in 1793 revived the sagging cotton industry in the South and made cotton farming profitable. The increase in production generated more work for the factories of the North. By the late 1800s assembly line production and interchangeable parts had been introduced; the telephone had replaced the telegraph. In addition, steam engines that drove machinery could be replaced by internal combustion engines, which had an efficiency rate about seven times greater than the steam engines.

By the beginning of the twentieth century, the Industrial Age had reached maturity in the United States. Steam power was slowly put to rest after the discovery of electricity. Not only could existing machinery in the factories be run by electricity, but also completely new machines were invented that relied on electricity—radios, automobiles, and later, vacuum tubes, airplanes, and televisions. Some of these technological wonders would eventually make the Information Age possible.

The Industrial Age brought with it a new class of the wealthy: businessmen. Rather than owning land, wealth came from two assets: the physical factory building with its machinery and the raw materials used to produce goods. The valued skills were organization, planning, directing the workforce, and supervising the production of goods.

Running a factory required new management techniques. Instead of the family-run businesses of the past, the workforce became a diverse mix of people moving into the city, both U.S. citizens and recent immigrants. The management structure became a top-down, hierarchical relationship creating two classes with a clear division of labor: white-collar workers (management) and blue-collar workers (labor).

The economy, now supply-driven, operated differently. Instead of the one-to-one relationship of supplier to one local market, the Industrial Age economy operated under

A steam locomotive at Scotland's Firth of Forth bridge in 1914.

a one-to-many model of one supplier to many markets. For example, car manufacturers sent cars to dealerships; drugs were distributed through drugstores. Marketing developed as a cross between science, using census and other data for population distribution and identification, and psychology, making educated guesses at what people wanted and were most likely to buy. Technological developments in transportation (trains, steamships, and automobiles) facilitated the distribution of mass-produced goods nationwide.

The Information Age (1960 into the Twenty-first Century)

The beginning of the Information Age in the United States marked the convergence of two developments. In 1956 white-collar jobs outnumbered blue-collar jobs for the first time. About this same time computer technology advanced, making computers smaller, faster, and less expensive. Mixing educated business leaders, scientists, and statisticians with readily available computational machines created new potential for doing business. Whereas machines in the

Industrial Age helped humankind overcome physical limitations, computer-aided technologies in the Information Age help overcome mental limitations.

Overcoming mental limitations can create new information, but that information is useless unless it is shared. The next key development in the Information Age was the networked computer. Networks—the Internet, for example—allowed access to the new information and created new channels for distribution of services. Now business interactions could take place on a many-to-many basis. Many suppliers could reach many markets. This was especially true for those companies that are strictly service companies—Wal-Mart, for instance. Wal-Mart, which is basically a discount distribution center for many kinds of goods, has mastered the many-to-many business transaction. It uses a just-in-time

inventory system networked to its entire distribution system. As a result, everyone in the supply line, from the store employees to the vendors, can determine the status of any product.

In addition to transforming existing businesses, technological changes have also opened up entirely new business opportunities. A prime example is the online auction site, e-Bay. E-Bay is one of the few dot-com companies that turned a profit almost from the start; e-Bay puts many sellers in contact with many buyers in a way that was not possible before.

The primary source of wealth in the Information Age is knowledge. So-called knowledge workers are in high demand, as are those managers who have the ability to facilitate teamwork in the new workplace environment. Entrepreneurial knowledge workers have the potential to make millions

Hasbro workers on a toy assembly line in Pawtucket, Rhode Island, in 1990.

or even billions of dollars from their ideas. Independent knowledge workers in the upper echelons of their craft command high salaries in corporations and other businesses. Businesses that can attract knowledge workers and incorporate them into innovative teams also have the potential to make billions of dollars. Human capital is an information company's biggest asset.

As happened in the Industrial Age, business management evolved in an attempt to keep pace with technological changes. Cooperation and teamwork began to replace the hierarchical structure of management. As the corporation replaced the factory, the old, bureaucratic style of management could not respond quickly enough to the fast-paced changes in technology. Smaller, flexible teams that work independently and have control of their work are required to meet that kind of demand. Product managers (often called team facilitators or team leaders) have to trust their staff to make multiple business decisions that affect the company's bottom line. The most valued skills in the Information Age are rapid learning, initiative, and teamwork.

A Demand-Driven Economy

Throughout the Industrial Age, the economy was supply driven. Business owners determined what products were made and how they were distributed. Internal operations were geared to efficiency and economies of scale, with marketing aimed at getting consumers to buy new products.

With access to the Internet, consumers can more easily shop around for products, reviewing the same product at many vendors or discovering even better alternatives sold by many vendors across the globe. If price is of primary concern, then the consumer buys the cheapest version of the product available. Not all consumers are price shoppers, however; businesses can benefit from online services by offering greater customization of their products so customers can adapt a product to fit their specific needs. This kind of offering creates a demand-driven economy where customers and consumers determine

Technology Standards

Implementing new technologies would not be effective without standards. In the United States, the Technology Administration (TA), a division of the Department of Commerce, performs that role. TA has three agencies through which it offers oversight, develops standards, and participates in the development of technology. These agencies are not so much interested in control as in setting standards in the interest of spreading technology quickly and in reviewing and supporting development in the national interest. The TA's three agencies:

- The Office of Technology Policy has the explicit mission of developing and advocating national policies and initiatives that use technology to build U.S. economic strength.
- The National Institute of Standards and Technology promotes economic growth and improves the quality of life by working with industry to develop and apply technology, measurements, and standards.
- The National Technical Information Service collects and disseminates scientific, technical, engineering, and related business information produced by the U.S. government and foreign sources.

what products are sold. Consequently, business success is measured by product effectiveness and a company's ability to respond quickly to market changes.

Businesses that use the Internet or an internal customer database have an additional advantage. They have a means of collecting consumer intelligence. When customer preferences change, such businesses know about it. They can compare the purchasing and browsing habits of all their customers to discover subtle changes in the market. Using technology will give businesses an edge on the competition, whether local or global.

One drawback to a demand-driven economy is the potential for becoming complacent—responding only to customer demands instead of pursuing truly innovative solutions. Historically, in the technology sector, the demand has always been for smaller, faster, and cheaper. True innovation requires thinking about new ways to solve problems versus making existing solutions better. Most customers do not have the technological vision to ask for a specific solution.

Regulation and Protection

The open exchange of information required in the Information Age requires somewhat open computer systems. Open systems can be vulnerable to attack, for example, information

Industries Producing Information Technology

Hardware Industries
✓ Computers and equipment
✓ Wholesale trade of computers and equipment
✓ Retail trade of computers and equipment
✓ Calculating and office machines
✓ Magnetic and optical recording media
✓ Electronic tubes
✓ Print circuit boards
✓ Semiconductors
✓ Passive electronic components
✓ Industrial instruments for measurement
✓ Instruments for measuring electricity
✓ Laboratory analysis instruments

Communications Equipment Industries
✓ Household audio and video equipment
✓ Telephone and telegraph equipment
✓ Radio and TV communications equipment

Software and Services Industries
✓ Computer programming services
✓ Prepackaged software
✓ Wholesale trade in software
✓ Retail trade in software
✓ Computer-integrated system design
✓ Computer processing, data preparation
✓ Information retrieval services
✓ Computer services management
✓ Computer rental and leasing
✓ Computer maintenance and repair
✓ Computer-related services

Communications Service Industries
✓ Telephone and telegraph communications
✓ Radio and TV broadcasting

Note: Based on SIC (Standard Industrial Classification) categories.
Source: Department of Commerce, Economics, and Statistics Administration, "Electronic Commerce: Information Technology Industries," *Digital Economy 2000.*

theft or viruses. Development of protective software is typically just behind the release of new technology.

The global economy affects both national and international policies on copyrights, taxation, and free speech. No one person, business, or country owns the Internet, thus no one has total control over commerce or the implementation of technological advances. Governments can regulate use somewhat within their countries, but most existing laws are insufficient to handle the complexities of a worldwide economy. For example, copyright laws permit fair use, allowing small portions of a work to be copied under certain conditions. However, with computer technology, the small portions currently allowed can be duplicated and redistributed thousands of times. This kind of distribution goes far beyond the original intent of the law.

Taxation creates another problem. Within the United States, state sales tax is paid only to businesses that are registered within that state. Most states have an honor system that requires taxpayers to voluntarily pay taxes on untaxed goods purchased in another state. Currently, many states are losing revenue on purchases made over the Internet. The same problem exists at the international level. Many European countries have a value-added tax on goods and services. They are unable to collect these taxes on Internet transactions. No one has yet devised a suitable and efficient way to collect such revenue for the taxing authorities.

How Much Is Too Much?
Technology is morally neutral, but it gives rise to some interesting moral dilemmas. There is a difference between wisdom and information, and knowledge lies somewhere between. In an Information Age where technology advances at an ever-increasing speed, one can easily forget wisdom in the pursuit of information. For example, technology makes us more efficient, but are we taking the right actions? Visionaries of the Industrial Age like H. G. Wells predicted that as technology advanced, humans would become machinelike. Although we are not becoming like machines, we are relying on them more heavily for routine interactions in our lives. The pervasiveness of technology

throughout society can easily lead to sloppy thinking or even nonthinking, blurring the lines between right and wrong.

For example, when collecting marketing data, how much is too much? At what point does electronic data collection become an invasion of privacy? The question arises because the information bits are scattered across many entities and no single data collection point has too much information. However, some companies troll the data collections of various agencies and businesses, collecting hundreds of bits of information about a person.

Computer technology has enabled us to copy text, music, movies, and other copyrighted material from the Internet without much fear of repercussions, even though such copying is illegal. Often, our only guide is our moral will. Without an underpinning of moral training and ethical behavior, technology itself will dictate what is right and wrong.

These observations indicate that another valued skill of the Information Age will be the ability to resist certain technological advances while embracing others. Although technology itself may be morally neutral, the changes it brings about are not. Integrity, character, and standards of behavior will be severely tested as the Information Age progresses.

Further Reading

Castells, Manuel. *The Power of Identity*. Malden, Mass.: Blackwell Publishers, 1997.

Dhillon, Gurpreet S., ed. *Social Responsibility in the Information Age: Issues and Controversies*. Hershey, Pa.: Idea Group Publishing, 2002.

Hunter, Richard. *World without Secrets: Business, Crime, and Privacy in the Age of Ubiquitous Computing*. New York: John Wiley & Sons, 2002.

Naisbett, John, and Patricia Aburdene. *Megatrends 2000*. New York: Avon Books, 1991.

Toffler, Alvin, and Heidi Toffler. *Creating a New Civilization: The Politics of the Third Wave*. Atlanta, Ga.: Turner Publishing, 1994.

Zey, Michael G. *Seizing the Future: How the Coming Revolution in Science, Technology, and Industry Will Expand the Frontiers of Human Potential and Reshape the Planet*. New York: Simon & Schuster, 1994.

—*Stephanie Buckwalter*

In 2000 Metallica founder Lars Ulrich, left, and Byrds cofounder Roger McGuinn testified before a Senate Judiciary Committee on digital music. Many musicians regard digital copying as a threat to their livelihoods.

Telecommuni-cations Industry

Once encompassing only telephone and telegraph businesses, the telecommunications industry has expanded dramatically since the 1980s as technology has provided new means for transmitting person-to-person communications electronically. Today telephone lines transmit faxes, electronic mail, video images, and computer data, and the telecommunications industry overlaps with the Internet and cable television industries.

The telecommunications industry has been profoundly affected by government regulation. The telephone sector of the industry has undergone radical restructuring as a result of changes in regulatory policy and practice; these changes have fostered a new climate of competition and innovation throughout the telecommunications industry.

Short History of the Telecommunications Industry

The telecommunications industry generates approximately $700 billion in annual revenues in the United States alone. Ironically, the inventor of the first working telecommunications device had a lot of trouble convincing people that it would make money.

In 1835 Samuel Morse, an artist, perfected a working telegraph. His invention would seem primitive today: it could broadcast only long or short electrical pulses, and Morse had to devise a code to use the pulses to transmit a message. At the time, however, Morse's invention seemed futuristic. It was claimed that his telegraph machine could transmit a message over a long distance almost instantly—a notion sure to evoke skepticism in an era when most people traveled by horse.

Overcoming this skepticism took time, but after eight years Morse convinced the U.S. Congress to build an experimental telegraph line from Washington, D.C., to Baltimore, Maryland. When the line was completed in 1844, Morse transmitted the first long-distance telecommunication; its message was "What hath God wrought?" As promised, the message traveled with lightning speed. The demonstration helped to establish the telegraph machine in the eyes of the public, and demand for telegraph

A Western Union messenger in Norfolk, Virginia, in 1911.

services grew. By the end of the nineteenth century, telegraph companies like Western Union had emerged as giants in the telecommunications industry.

Even then, however, the telegraph faced stiff competition from a newer technology—the telephone. Invented in 1876 by Alexander Graham Bell, a teacher of deaf students, the telephone carried the sound of a person's voice directly across great distances, and it required no coding. Like Morse, Bell had patented his invention, and he founded Bell Telephone—later, American Telephone & Telegraph Company; later still, AT&T Corporation—a year after he invented it.

Unlike Morse, Bell did not have a long wait before people realized that his invention had commercial potential. Indeed, several companies—including the formidable Western Union—attempted to enter the telephone business as competitors, only to be held off by Bell's patents. When those patents expired in the 1890s, however, several competitors did come forward, capturing a majority share of the market from AT&T. In response, AT&T began buying its smaller competitors. In 1910, in a demonstration of the dominance of the new technology, AT&T obtained a controlling interest in Western Union, which had begun to falter.

Invoking the Sherman Antitrust Act of 1890, the U.S. federal government forced AT&T to shed its interest in Western Union in 1913. In the 1920s and 1930s, however, the government gradually exempted telephone service from the scope of the Sherman Act, promulgating regulations by which AT&T and other local telephone service providers would not compete with one another for customers. This regulatory shift enabled AT&T to gain monopoly power in the market for long-distance telephone service and telephone equipment.

In exchange, AT&T—which became popularly known as Ma Bell—agreed to conduct its business as if it were a public utility. It created, for example, a telephone network that was very reliable and could be used for emergency communication. In

addition, it took on responsibility for making telephone service universally available, building telephone lines to unprofitable rural areas and then subsidizing service to those areas by charging other users higher rates. By the mid-1970s more than 90 percent of American homes had telephones.

AT&T's monopoly status had drawbacks, however. When Ma Bell held sway, the public saw little in the way of new telecommunications products and services. Preventing competition did not just keep other telephone companies from entering the market, it also eliminated the

Employees of Northwestern Telephone perch on a telephone pole in Houlton, Wisconsin, in 1914.

	Cellular Telephone Industry 1990 to 2000								
	Unit	1990	1994	1995	1996	1997	1998	1999	2000
Subscribers	Thousands	5,283	24,134	33,786	44,043	55,312	69,209	86,047	109,478
Service revenue	Millions of dollars	4,548	14,229	19,081	23,635	27,486	33,133	40,018	52,466
Average monthly bill	Dollars	80.90	56.21	51.00	47.70	42.78	39.43	41.24	45.27

Source: Cellular Telecommunications & Internet Association, *Semiannual Wireless Survey*, Washington, D.C., 2000.

incentive that fosters innovation in competitive markets.

AT&T itself had little incentive to invest in technology that would bring costs down because regulators would expect cost savings to be passed along to consumers in the form of lower rates. Regulators also blocked efforts by AT&T to leverage its expertise into new businesses, further stifling creativity. In this regulatory climate AT&T was able to implement some innovations, for example, touch-tone dialing in the 1960s, but the innovations were aimed primarily at enabling AT&T to handle more phone calls over its existing copper-wire network without having to lay new wires. In its approach to consumer-oriented services, AT&T was even less innovative. It did not offer telephones in any color other than black, for example, until 1955. Customers could not seek colored telephones from other suppliers, as no other suppliers existed.

During the 1960s and 1970s, AT&T increasingly came under fire by consumer advocates who charged that its monopoly led to higher prices for consumers. In 1974 the U.S. Justice Department filed a lawsuit seeking the breakup of AT&T. In a settlement of this lawsuit a decade later, AT&T was split apart and the entire telephone industry was restructured. AT&T became a long-distance telephone service and equipment manufacturing company; these sectors of the market were opened to competition. Local and regional telephone service providers retained their monopolies, but they were spun off into seven companies known as the Baby Bells, each of which was granted a monopoly on service in a specific geographic area.

Initially the breakup caused confusion among consumers, most of whom had to deal for the first time with two telephone companies instead of one. By the mid-1990s, however, competition in the long-distance and equipment-manufacturing areas was robust, and prices for consumers had fallen. Abolishing the long-distance service monopoly appeared to have worked, and the Baby Bells—restricted from entering nonmonopoly businesses as long as they held on to their local and regional monopolies—were eager to expand.

The Modern Telecommunications Industry

The breakup of AT&T was not the only profound change within the telecommunications industry. Technological advances played a part. Telephone lines had once been used only for voice calls, but by the 1990s inexpensive fax machines were using more and more lines to transmit documents. Likewise, the development of powerful, low-cost computers had more and more businesses—and even homes—using modems to access private networks or the Internet to transmit data and e-mail. Cellular telephones, first developed commercially in the mid-1980s, were also becoming increasingly affordable.

Perhaps the most significant advance, however, was the invention of a new kind of line to replace the copper wire that had been used to transmit phone calls since the days of Alexander Graham Bell. Fiber-optic lines, which carry information as a beam of light rather than an electrical signal, were first developed for telephone use in the mid-1980s. Fiber-optic lines can carry far more information than can copper wires;

indeed, a high-quality fiber-optic network can transmit cable television, video images, the Internet, and voice simultaneously—a phenomenon known in the industry as convergence.

To reflect the changing technological environment, Congress in 1996 passed a new telecommunications act. Intended to open all aspects of telecommunications to competition, it significantly relaxed many restrictions on the operations and corporate structure of the Baby Bells. Reflecting the new networking technology, the law allowed telephone-service providers to offer cable television service; it also allowed cable television providers and companies in other industries to offer telephone service.

Under the Telecommunications Act of 1996, the Baby Bells could immediately offer long-distance service outside the geographic area in which they held a local and regional service monopoly. They could not, however, offer such service within their home areas until they had demonstrated to federal regulators that they had completely opened their local and regional networks to competitors.

Working on satellite dishes in New York state in 1992.

A Bedouin man uses his cell phone in 1996.

The passage of this act spurred a flurry of activity among telecommunications companies. The Baby Bells—once considered stolid and unexciting—entered into several mergers with one another and with long-distance carriers, ultimately consolidating into four large companies offering a wide range of services: Verizon Communications, SBC Communications, BellSouth Corp., and Qwest Communications International. Telecommunications companies made forays into cable television and Internet services, and cellular telephones became an increasingly important consumer product. Makers of telecommunications gear—such as fiber-optics networks—split off or developed

independently from providers of telecommunications services. A host of new companies entered the industry, largely seeking corporate clients that wanted to build their own telecommunications networks.

Adding to the frenzy, which became increasingly intense toward the end of the 1990s, was the rapid rise in Internet usage. The demand—and the projected demand—for high-speed Internet access led to a boom in telecommunications investment and spending as companies built new networks and upgraded old ones. The proliferation of commercial Web sites, which required specialized telecommunications equipment to handle large volumes of visitors, further enlarged the sector.

New networks were expensive: from 1996 to 2000 telecommunications companies increased their capital spending 25 percent each year, on average, reaching a total of $124 billion in 2000. Many smaller telecommunications companies were losing money building expensive fiber-optic or cellular networks, but investors seemed willing to make up the difference in hopes that demand for new services would ultimately make the investment in new networks worthwhile.

In 2000 the Internet investment bubble burst, with commercial Web sites folding by the dozen and many firms going bankrupt. The telecommunications investment bubble burst soon afterward, as investors pulled their money out of the sector. Contributing to the decline was a lack of demand for high-speed Internet services, especially in residential markets. As of 2001 not even 5 percent of U.S. homes had high-speed Internet access. Much of the capacity of the expensive fiber-optic networks developed in the late 1990s was never used. Smaller telecommunications companies that had borrowed large sums of money went bankrupt; others laid off thousands of workers.

Future of the Telecommunications Industry

Despite the stark reversal of fortunes experienced by some telecom companies in

2000 and 2001, most industry observers think that, over the long term, convergence will become a reality. Even now the industry is far from finished; the Baby Bells, for example, have so far weathered the hard times relatively well.

Their good fortune, however, is generally attributed to their continuing monopoly on local telephone service in most states. Indeed, the lack of competition in local telephone markets is widely considered to be the most dramatic failure of the Telecommunications Act of 1996. By 2001 only 3.2 percent of residences and small businesses nationwide received local phone service from a company other than a Baby Bell. The Federal Communications Commission, which oversees telecommunications, has declared local service competitive in only seven states.

In contrast, regional telephone service has generally been opened to competition. Large corporate clients that can provide a telephone company with enough revenue to justify the cost of building lines to their offices generally have their pick of service providers.

Why the persistent lack of competition at the local level? The reasons are complex, differing from state to state, but basically the Baby Bells own the local networks and would-be competitors must buy access from them to provide local service to homes and small businesses. Competitors complain that the Baby Bells charge more for access to the local network than a competitor can charge for residential service. The Baby Bells argue that artificially low rate caps placed on local residential service by regulators in many states are to blame.

The lack of competition in local service clearly seems to be imposing costs on consumers. From the time of AT&T's breakup in 1984 to 2001, the price of long-distance service has fallen by 34 percent, but the price of local telephone service has increased by 70 percent. In New York, the first state to declare local service competitive, consumers have saved approximately $700 million in service charges since 1999—about $300 million on long-distance service and $400 million on local service.

The slow pace of opening local markets to competition has led to calls for yet another radical restructuring of the telecommunications industry, this time by splitting each of the Baby Bells into two companies, one that would own the local network and one that would provide local telephone service. Perhaps the telecommunications industry will face such restructuring, or perhaps another new technology will emerge and rock the industry to its core again. What seems certain is that the industry will not stand still.

Careers in the Telecommunications Industry

As the telecommunications industry has evolved from a focus on telephones to a broad-based industry incorporating Internet services, wireless communication, and cable television, career opportunities in the field have likewise expanded. According to the U.S. Department of Labor, in 2000 the telecommunications industry employed approximately 1.2 million workers.

The telecommunications industry employs engineers (including electrical and computer engineers, as well as network systems analysts), salespeople (retail and wholesale), and office support staff. Telephone craft workers—about 22 percent of people employed by the industry—install, repair, and maintain telephone equipment, cable and access lines, and telecommunications systems. Their work also includes managing the complex switching and dialing equipment used in central offices and solving network-related problems.

Jobs in the telecommunications industry vary widely in terms of skills and training requirements. Many require on-the-job training in specific skills that may take years to master completely. Employers require a college degree for many managerial and professional jobs. Most companies prefer to hire craft workers with training in electronics; familiarity with computers is also important. Training sources include two- and four-year college programs in electronics or communications, trade schools, and training provided by equipment and software manufacturers.

Further Reading

Brooks, John. *Telephone: The First Hundred Years.* New York: Harper & Row, 1976.

Cole, Barry G., ed. *After the Breakup: Assessing the New Post–AT&T Divestiture Era.* New York: Columbia University Press, 1991.

Crandall, Robert W., and Leonard Waverman. *Who Pays for Universal Service? When Telephone Subsidies Become Transparent.* Washington, D.C.: Brookings Institution Press, 2000.

Rosenbush, Steve, and Peter Elstrom. "Eight Lessons from the Telecom Mess." *BusinessWeek,* Aug. 13, 2001, 60–67.

Saracco, Roberto, et al. *The Disappearance of Telecommunications.* New York: IEEE Press, 2000.

—*Mary Sisson*

See also:
Freelancing; Technology.

Telecommuting

Telecommuting refers to the use of information and communication technologies to enable work to be done at sites away from a traditional workplace. Although telecommuting often takes place in the home, it can use a variety of flexible locales, including satellite offices and neighborhood telework centers. The term *telework* is often used interchangeably with telecommuting.

Telecommuting varies: some employees telecommute full-time, but more and more employees are choosing to skip the commute to work one or more days a week. Instead of traveling to their primary workplace, they keep in touch with the home office via an assortment of telecommunications technologies. According to the International Telework Association and Council, an industry group in Washington, D.C., more than 16.5 million people in the United States, or about 12 percent of the workforce, worked at home one or more days a month in 2001. Slightly more than 17 percent, or 2.8 million, of these were new telecommuters; 9.3 million U.S. workers telecommute at least one full day per week.

Jack Nilles has been described as the father of telecommuting. Nilles coined the term in the 1970s in response to developing strategies for dealing with the energy crisis that the United States was experiencing—in particular, as a way to ameliorate the traffic congestion in southern California. Telecommuting can be seen as a mechanism to reduce traffic congestion and air pollution. Futurist Alvin Toffler also foresaw the importance of telecommuting, which he discussed in his influential work, *The Third Wave* (1980).

Why Telecommute?

Telecommuting has been increasingly promoted as a workplace option with benefits for both the employer and the employee. In a tight labor market, many companies offer flexible work arrangements to attract and retain employees. For the employer, telecommuting is attractive because it promotes organizational flexibility and reduces the cost of office space in high-cost and crowded locales. Employers can ensure that the workforce is happier and more productive and are able to hire the best people for the job, regardless of their location. For the employee, telecommuting can be attractive because it reduces commute time and other costs (clothing and meals, for example), provides a better balance of work and family life, and increases productivity. It particularly benefits workers with specific disabilities.

Telecommuting has proved to be very popular among parents with small children, because working at home allows them to be with their children and to work. With telecommuting, workers are able to enjoy the benefits of a full-time job while not sacrificing time with their children. This peace of mind has made many of those parents valuable assets for their employers, because these employees tend

Wage and Salary Workers Paid for Job-related Work Done at Home
1997
(in thousands)

Occupational Group	
Professional specialty	969
Executive, administrative, and managerial	867
Sales occupations	640
Administrative support, including clerical	611
Service occupations	256
Precision production, craft, and repair	116
Technicians and related support	112
Operators, fabricators, and laborers	73
Industry	
Services	1,616
Manufacturing	517
Wholesale trade	343
Finance, insurance, and real estate	330
Retail trade	289
Transportation and public utilities	205
Public administration	196
Construction	136

Benefits of Telecommuting

For Employer	For Employee
• Contributes to company profits • Promotes organizational flexibility • Reduces cost of office space • Ensures happier, more productive workforce • Enables firms to hire best people for the job regardless of their location	• Provides increased flexibility • Reduces commuting time • Reduces cost • Reduces stress • Increases productivity • Limits some types of distractions • Provides better balance of work and family life

to work harder to keep their telecommuting status.

Indeed, several studies by business magazines and journals have shown that telecommuting has increased overall employee productivity and effectiveness. Employees who telecommute have been found to take fewer sick days and to have much higher morale, which can keep employee turnover low. Telecommuting takes self-discipline. An employee sometimes needs a few weeks or longer to become adjusted to new surroundings and new schedules.

Challenges in Telecommuting

The importance of self-discipline points to one of the main dangers for telecommuters—the threat of distraction. The television, the morning paper, and various personal chores all compete for the telecommuter's attention and time. Although telecommuting is popular among people with young children, many companies ask employees to arrange for child care during work hours before allowing parents to telecommute.

One potential solution is the telework center, which is gaining popularity in some parts of the country. Telework centers provide computers, Internet connections, and other standard office features such as photocopiers and fax machines. Teleworkers can still work closer to home, while also being surrounded by a productivity-inspiring office environment.

Other challenges to telecommuters include the sense of isolation brought about by working at home. Telework centers might serve to ameliorate this problem. Also, telecommuting is sometimes hard for supervisors and managers; many feel they cannot adequately supervise employees they cannot see. For them trust becomes an issue; until they grow to trust the employees who are telecommuting, they will be suspicious about employees who want to work at home.

Most telecommuters begin in their jobs as on-site workers. After proving themselves to be valuable employees, they enter into telecommuting work arrangements. Only rarely do employers hire new workers as telecommuters. In some large corporations, the decision to allow telecommuting is sometimes left to individual managers.

Principles of Telecommuting

As the Internet becomes more ubiquitous, more people will use it to increase the efficacy of telecommuting and for occasional telecommuting. Because many forms of work are not suited for telecommuting, it will not become a social or economic imperative. However, a social and legal framework for telecommuting that considers the best conditions for workers must be developed in the United States.

An example of such a framework is the European Union's wide agreement on guidelines for telecommuting in the commerce sector. Twelve principles for telecommuting have been elaborated, including those applying to health and safety at the home site. The principles state that telecommuting should be voluntary; suitable to the individual, the work, and the environment; and subject to the appropriate collective rights agreements that apply to other employees. They also state that all equipment needed for the job will be provided, installed, and maintained by the employer, while additional costs accrued by the worker to meet job duties will be considered by the employer. Finally, to decrease the isolating effects of telecommuting, workers should have appropriate access to company information, as well as opportunities to meet regularly with colleagues.

—*Leslie Regan Shade*

Networking technology has enabled people in a wide variety of occupations to work without leaving home.

For example, at Xerox Corporation, managers are empowered to determine the appropriateness of telecommuting in their individual business units.

Companies that have been successful with large-scale telecommuting programs have provided training, both for the employees and their supervisors, to make sure everyone understands what is expected. Employees who have been telecommuting for several years have reported that their jobs are easier when they know they have the trust of their employer.

Employment experts predict that more people will want to telecommute in the future; these experts say that the numbers will increase each year because telecommuting saves companies money and allows them to retain valuable employees. Wireless connectivity will allow more devices to communicate both without cables and regardless of location, which is expected to lead to more and more employees choosing to telecommute. Indeed, some have argued that the ability to telecommute will prompt an exodus from urban areas, a view that Bill Gates, for example, put forward in his 1995 book *The Road Ahead*. A mass migration from the cities has not yet occurred. Gates has subsequently argued that as people commonly overestimate change in the short term and underestimate it in the long term, the profound social changes to be wrought by telecommuting lie in the future.

Further Reading

EuroCommerce and UNI-Europa. "European Agreement on Guidelines on Telework in Commerce." http://www.telework-mirti.org/uni.doc (March 18, 2003).

Gates, Bill, with Nathan Myhrvold, and Peter Rinearson. *The Road Ahead.* New York: Viking, 1995.

Jackson, Paul J., and Jos M. van der Wielen, eds. *Teleworking—International Perspectives: From Telecommuting to the Virtual Organization.* London: Routledge, 1998.

Nilles, Jack M. *Managing Telework: Strategies for Managing the Virtual Workforce.* New York: John Wiley & Sons, 1998.

Toffler, Alvin. *The Third Wave.* New York: Bantam Books, 1987.

—John Riddle and Leslie Regan Shade

Glossary

arbitration Method of resolving disputes by use of a neutral third party to hear arguments and make a ruling. See encyclopedia entry.

balance sheet Document that summarizes the assets and liabilities of a business at a given time. See encyclopedia entry.

broadband A range of communication methods, including cell phone, cable, and satellite, among others.

brokerage Business that sells investment vehicles and advice. See encyclopedia entry, Security Industry.

capital Money or wealth that is put at risk to fund a business enterprise. See encyclopedia entry.

cash flow analysis Process of examining the financial effects of different decisions. See encyclopedia entry, Cash Flow.

cobranding Cooperation between at least two companies to sell or market a product or product line.

collective bargaining Negotiations between management and a union to establish a labor contract. See encyclopedia entry.

conglomerate A company that grows by merging with or buying businesses in several different industries.

connectivity Degree to which computer systems can interact with each other.

cooperative Corporation owned either by its employees or customers; credit unions are an example of a cooperative business.

copyright The exclusive ownership rights of authors, artists, or corporations to their works. See encyclopedia entry.

credit A promise to pay. See encyclopedia entry.

credit union Nonprofit financial institution owned by its members that functions as a bank.

day trading Buying and selling stocks at a very rapid pace; usually done in the course of a day or one week. See encyclopedia entry.

disability insurance Public payments made to individuals who are unable to work because of physical or mental disabilities.

economies of scale Declining average cost of production that results from increasing output. See encyclopedia entry.

entrepreneur Person who combines different resources to make goods or services available to others. See encyclopedia entry, Entrepreneurship.

franchise License to operate a business that is part of a larger chain. See encyclopedia entry.

globalization Expansion of international trade and increasing financial links between nations. See encyclopedia entry.

guild Association of individuals, usually skilled in a trade or craft, created for the mutual aid of its members. See encyclopedia entry, Labor Union.

income statement Statement used by a business to report and assess its financial performance. See encyclopedia entry.

incorporate Legal process of becoming a corporation. See encyclopedia entry, Corporation.

independent contractor Self-employed person who offers services to the public. See encyclopedia entry, Freelancing.

inflation Period of rising prices. See encyclopedia entry.

insider trading Buying or selling stock based on information not publicly available.

interchangeable parts Components used in the production process that are identical. See encyclopedia entry.

monetary policy Government's use of its power over the money supply to influence economic growth and inflation. See encyclopedia entry.

monopoly Type of market that involves only one seller. See encyclopedia entry.

nationalization Government takeover of private industries.

partnership Business structure with two or more individuals as owners. See encyclopedia entry.

procurement Process of businesses buying the materials they need.

quota A predetermined limit on the amount of foreign goods that can enter a country.

racketeering Conducting a business using dishonest or criminal methods.

shareholder Person who owns stock in a corporation. See encyclopedia entries, Investment; Stocks and Bonds.

sole proprietorship A business owned by one person.

standard deviation Statistical measure of the range of an investment's performance; the higher the number, the riskier the investment.

standard of living Quality of life. See encyclopedia entry.

stock options Right of employees (granted by employer) to buy shares in a company at a certain price at some point in the future.

subsidy Government financial support of a business endeavor. See encyclopedia entry.

trade union Association of workers created to improve their pay and working conditions. See encyclopedia entry, Labor Union.

transnational corporation Corporation that operates in many different countries. See encyclopedia entry, Multinational Corporation.

Treasury bills (T-bills) Bonds issued by the U.S. government.

venture capital Private funds used to start or expand a business. See encyclopedia entry.

welfare (or public assistance) Public assistance to the poor, which may include money payments, job training, food, and other benefits.

workers' compensation Publicly funded payments made to workers injured on the job.

Index

Page numbers in **boldface** type indicate article titles. Page numbers in *italic* type indicate illustrations or other graphics.